VIRTUALLY SUCCESSFUL

simple ways for virtual assistants to find (and keep) clients

CINDY GREENWAY

WWW.GROWYOURVABIZ.COM

Foreword by Andrea J. Lee

Virtually Successful: Simple Ways for Virtual Assistants to Find (And Keep) Clients

ISBN: 978-0-9809086-0-2

Printed in the United States of America

Dedication

This book is dedicated to those who have supported me since 2003 – my family, my friends, my business partners, my past and current clients and my Virtual Assistant colleagues.

To my husband, Kevin and two sons, Nico and Jacob, for their patience, support and for believing in me. I love that my business has given me the flexibility to be with you.

To my Mom, Natalia, & Dad, Joao, for teaching me the value of hard work and commitment. I am who I am now because of how you raised me. To my Mother-in-Law, Shannon and Father-in-Law, David, for their support and for looking after my sons so I could get work done!

To my business partners Tina Forsyth and Andrea Lee, for reaching out and partnering with me to create what I was afraid to build on my own. To Tina for brainstorming with me and keeping me grounded (and for putting a little fire under my butt at times!). To Andrea for her ongoing belief and encouragement. I treasure our partnership and look forward to it lasting far beyond this journey.

Sylva Leduc, you were the start to my skill development and business growth. You believed in me and openly shared with me in so many ways. You saw in me what I didn't see in myself for years…you were right! Stephen Fairley, you challenge me in so many ways and give me the freedom to build, explore and manage more than I thought possible. I am grateful for the appreciation you show me, and the trust you have in me.

Mike Flannery, my editor, for your patience and allowing me to vent during my first experience with writing (and rewriting!) this book. Thank you!

To all my past and current clients, for giving me the opportunity to learn, create and support you while also enjoying the success of your own business growth. And to all the Virtual Assistants I have connected with over the years - thank you for giving me the opportunity to share with you. My hope is that what I have learned will impact you as positively as it has impacted me.

Foreword

As you prepare to read this book, 'Virtually Successful: Simple Steps for Virtual Assistants to Get (and Keep) Clients' by my colleague and friend Cindy Greenway, there is something you need to know. It's a simple thing but quite significant.

People - all kinds of people - get GREAT around Cindy. Period.

What do I mean by that? Well, let's start with clients. You don't need to look far before you realize Cindy's virtual clients take a very big leap forward - in revenue, productivity and freedom - when Cindy comes on board as their Virtual Assistant. These days, she doesn't take on many new clients anymore, but the ones she maintains treat her like gold. Why?

Because she's like gold to them.

In fact, that's the story between the lines of this book. Sure the book tells you how to think differently about being a top-notch Virtual Assistant. In fact, I'll wager you'll finish this book more excited than before about what's possible. And yes, you'll also discover tools and methods to achieve not just the money you want to earn, but live the lifestyle you want. With Cindy showing you the way, you can't help but become GREAT yourself, and guess what? You too, will be like gold to your clients, because that's the thing Cindy can't help but pass onto you through these pages.

It's a popular saying that "You become like the people, thoughts and information you surround yourself with" and for that reason especially, I applaud you for your choice in this book about greatness.

Since 2004, I've had the honor of partnering with Cindy in a Virtual Assistant matching service for the self-help industry. Out of all the people with VA experience on the planet, I'll tell you a little story about why I knew Cindy would be the perfect partner in this. We met face-to-face for the first time at a conference in Vancouver, British Columbia, where Cindy was in attendance with a client. One of the presentation topics was 'How to Build a Team' and Cindy and her client were invited - spur of the moment - to sit in front of the room and be interviewed about what it was like to work with each other. The client talked about the benefits and challenges of having a VA and Cindy talked about her perspective.

Not only was the interview the highlight of the day, but it was clear-as-day (painfully clear, in fact, to some people) what a truly incredible asset Cindy was to this client. As a result of the interview, more than a handful of the other attendees immediately rushed up to her, demanding Cindy accept them as her next client, willing to pay top dollar for that privilege.

I'm proud and honored to be writing this foreword for Cindy, and invite you take a moment now to breathe deeply, relax your mind, and prepare to submerge yourself in the new thoughts Cindy's prepared on the pages that follow. Don't worry, it won't be difficult because Cindy keeps it real throughout. The material in these pages is results-oriented, useful and focused on the creation of value for your and your (potential) clients.

Follow the advice inside and you'll get where you want to go.

One last thing. It's my belief that Virtual Assistants are just beginning to understand the power they hold - to make or break the hundreds of thousands of business ventures born each year. In this book are the keys to wielding that power well, and doing it in a way that serves you, doesn't exhaust you, and puts a spring in your step.

Whether you like it or not, as a veteran or aspiring Virtual Assistant, you're playing a significant role in the history of work on this planet! The virtual, environmental, efficient world of online work is truly unique, the people who succeed in it are equally special and I know this book can only bring more recognition to the profession. These are exciting times indeed.

Looking back on Cindy's success, there's just one more observation I think is worth mentioning. That's the truly remarkable number of Virtual Assistants she's brought up through the ranks, and who are wildly successful now because of what they learned from her. That's the true mark of a leader and teacher, don't you think? Someone who not only gets and STAYS great themselves, but everyone around them can't help but get great too.

Read this book for a road map to sustainable success as a VA. You won't find a greater advocate for VA success anywhere else.

Best wishes from a former fellow Virtual Assistant,

a.

Andrea J. Lee
Author, *Pink Spoon Marketing & Multiple Streams of Coaching Income*

My Story

When I first started Victoria Business Solutions in 2003, I knew nothing about running a company. As a new Mom, my intention was to start up a secretarial services business and do small jobs. At the time I had never heard the term 'Virtual Assistant' or, 'VA'.

When I researched secretarial services on the Internet and came across a website for VA's, I was intrigued. I researched and read everything I could and also visited the websites of other VA's. I was excited. I knew I could do this: I had great administrative skills and, more importantly, I was committed and determined to contributing to my family and succeeding in this business.

At first, I started with small jobs on an, 'as needed' basis. I went on to receive various project contracts through local government. I also started working with small business owners, one project at a time. My business grew quickly. Over time I added more clients, took on more responsibility, created stronger relationships and built my expertise in several areas. Within just a few years, I found myself in a position where I was able to completely restructure my business, work exclusively with just a few highly respected clients and increase my revenue.

Before 2003, I had never even heard the terms autoresponders, shopping cart, payment gateway, 'Pink Spoon' marketing or article submission. I tell you this because, if you're new to the VA profession – there's no need to be discouraged. By committing to investing time in yourself, relationship building, developing your skills and changing old mindsets, you too can experience life-changing results.

I'm passionate about the VA industry and in supporting others who also want to build a successful VA business. I aspire to share what others may conceal. The opportunities far exceed the number of proficient and competent Virtual Assistants. The profession and clients await you.

About This Book

By far, the two most frequently asked questions I get from Virtual Assistants from around the world, are:

1. How do I get clients? And,
2. How do I keep clients?

This book is designed to answer these two critical questions and to provide you with the practical details to help you implement change within your own business. The tips and strategies you'll find in this book may seem like common sense, yet few Virtual Assistants actively practice them. If you use even a few of these tips I'm confident that you'll set yourself apart from the rest of the pack.

I have been fortunate to experience great success within the VA industry and am excited to share key strategies with you so you too can start, build and enjoy a rewarding and successful VA business.

As you read through this book, note I am sharing this information based on my research, my own personal experiences, from the work I have done with highly respected business owners, and from my conversations with over 500 business owners over the years. Certainly, this is not the only way to start a successful VA business, but it works – I'm proof of that.

WHY THIS BOOK AND WHY NOW

I've read a number of books related to the Virtual Assistant industry and many offer great tips on starting a VA business. After reading those books, however, I found they were missing a critical element. There were very few specific strategies offered that were designed to help the VA find and retain their ideal clients. The books that did offer some strategies seemed to miss one of the most important opportunities – to share specific, real-world examples and experiences of how to find and retain clients. That's why I wrote this book. I wanted to share with you practical, repeatable and proven strategies to show you what really works -- and what really doesn't work.

I've also investigated numerous training programs created specifically for Virtual Assistants. In many cases, I've been surprised at the content (and the cost) of these programs – if you are interested in learning about how to equip and supply your office or how to decorate your office environment, then these courses may be for you. But if you already know all the basics and want to learn the real business of being a Virtual Assistant -- save your money. Some of us require basic business skills training, for those of you who want to know more about how to build long-term client relationships and generate revenue – this book is for you.

If you go to Google and do a search for, "virtual assistant" you get 1,060,000 returns. This tells me the VA business is growing significantly, yet there are VAs around the globe that are struggling to find clients and there are business owners everywhere struggling to find the right VA. This means it is a great time with lots of opportunities to make a living as a Virtual Assistant – all you have to do is arm yourself with the right tools to help you become successful. That is where this book comes in to play.

Again, if you are looking for a 'how-to' book on naming your business, creating business brochures or setting up your home office this is not the book for you. There are plenty of generic business books out there that can help you decide what desk you need or what computer software you should buy. If you are looking for a book that speaks specifically to the challenges and opportunities for today's VA, then read on.

You'll also discover what an 'Ideal' client really is and learn exactly what it takes to find them – and what simple steps you can take to make sure you keep them. You'll learn how to do this using simple, specific and proven methods.

Remember, as a professional Virtual Assistant, you are now a business owner and industry professional. You are not a secretary or office assistant, sitting in an office receiving orders from a manager. YOU are your manager. You are now in a position where you need to represent yourself in a way that reflects your professionalism, skills and uniqueness. This book will tell you exactly how to do that.

WHAT TO TAKE AWAY FROM THIS BOOK

This book is about creating the business you want to create. It's about building your confidence, enhancing your business relation-ships and figuring out what type of client you want to work with. Ultimately, once you do that, you can work with professionals who value and respect you and who are grateful for your contribution to the success of their own business.

Within nine months of starting my business I was able to con-tinuously attract and retain great clients. Within two years of start-ing my business, I was a sought-after VA, with a solid reputation, and I had more clients than I knew what to do with. Within four years of starting my business my expertise was clearly defined and my reputation had soared. I decided who I wanted to work with and on what terms. Once my business reached a 'critical mass' I was able to cut back my client base, while increasing my profit. I want to show you how to do the same.

As you read the following chapters and learn the strategies, struggles and lessons of my own journey, I encourage you to make note of key details and apply them to your business. I'm confident that if you implement even a few simple tactics I suggest, you will set yourself far apart from your competitors and you will experience dramatic results.

The steps I included in this book are 'tried and true'. Though I firmly belive in every single one of the steps, if I were to identify the top three critical ingredients to success as a VA, they would be:

- Shifting your mindset from thinking of yourself as merely an employee, to the idea of being a self-reliant business owner and Virtual Assistant.
- Understanding your target market and the challenges they face.
- Taking inventory of your clients and applying your new mindset when connecting with potential and current clients.

These specific steps are critical in ensuring you get (and keep) the attention of your clients.

Let's get started!

Table of Contents

Before we begin, let's define the term Virtual Assistant.

The traditional definition of a Virtual Assistant is, "an independent contractor who provides assistance to other professionals, using technology such as email, Internet, fax, from their own home office." Boring! Besides, it doesn't really get at the heart at what VAs *really* do, does it?

Let me share with you my own definition of a Virtual Assistant:

"A Virtual Assistant is a professional independent contractor who provides expertise, skill and assistance to other professionals to help them build their business and generate more revenue."

More and more women around the world are choosing the Virtual Assistant profession for their career, however many are also experiencing frustration with building their business. According to a recent survey, published by 'Online Office Assistants', (www.OnlineOfficeAssistants.com) over 90% of current Virtual Assistants are women who plan to make the Virtual Assistant profession their new career.

One of the biggest mistakes new Virtual Assistants typically make is not selecting their target market.

Without a target market, a VA may experience extreme frustration in finding and retaining clients. By the end of this book, you will understand why this aspect is so critical.

CHAPTER ONE

Set Your Sights – How to Find Your Target Market

People ask me all the time, "Cindy, if you had to start all over again, what would be the one thing you would do differently?" My immediate response is, "I would define my target market from the start."

Identifying your target market is essential in the success of your business. According to VANetworking – the original Virtual Assistant Networking Forum (www.VANetworking.com) - only about 45% of VAs niche market themselves. My question is, what are the other 55% doing?

You can have the best looking website, great business cards and fabulous looking brochures however, without an identified target market, your information will be too general. It will be missing specific language your potential client needs to see in order to recognize the need for your services and gain an interest in learning more about you.

Experts say that you need to determine exactly who you plan on selling your services to. However, by selecting a specific target market, you may feel this will limit potential work, clients and revenue. Why do you need to select one or two specific markets to work with when you have the opportunity to work with numerous markets?

Here's the reality – by not targeting and promoting your services within a specific market, you are actually limiting yourself and preventing your business from growing. More on this below.

If you're having trouble with why or how to select a target market for your VA business, you are not alone. This is one of the most difficult decisions business owners face.

Let's consider the two options:

Not selecting a target market

Let's say, you decide not to select a target market, yet you offer great services, tremendous expertise and affordable rates. You promote yourself in various places, advertise in the yellow pages and local newspaper, attend all kinds of networking functions and experience very little return on your investments of time and money (i.e. no clients).

When you look back at your ad, you realize it is very generic. It doesn't speak to a specific audience and therefore it speaks to no one, really. That's the nature of general advertising. As a result, you receive very few phone calls because you didn't target anyone specific and it doesn't contain the language that attracts the clients you want.

Selecting a target market

Now let's say you select a target market – for example, female lawyers who specialize in personal injury law. You still offer great services, tremendous expertise and affordable rates. You research (and perhaps join) the various places online and offline where the attorneys gather. You determine the specific challenges the attorneys face and you clarify how your services address those challenges. All of your marketing material – website, brochures, business cards and verbal introduction, etc. - includes specific language these female attorneys will relate to. This will peak their interest in your services and show that you've done your homework.

Which of these two scenarios gives you a better opportunity to find new clients?

The second scenario provides a more favorable picture of what we would like to experience in order to meet new prospects and build relationships with them.

SELECTING YOUR TARGET MARKET

If you're starting your business from scratch, consider working with a target you are familiar with. For example, if you're familiar with the work of personal injury attorneys and you are confident you can support them in accomplishing their goals, why not consider that your target market? By selecting a profession you are already familiar with, you'll likely have the answers to the challenges they face, therefore making it easier to identify specifically how you can best support them.

As you build relationships and work with numerous members of your chosen market, you may find yourself specializing even further. For example, if you become very skilled in a solving a particular problem faced by your market and you enjoy this task, you may decide to remove other services from your list of offerings and specialize in this specific area. This allows you to focus your efforts even further.

My Story...

When I started my VA business, I told everyone about it. I remember speaking to a colleague who asked me, "Who is your target market?" My first reaction was, "I don't need a target market - everyone can benefit from my services."

I thought I had the whole package - a great website, professional business cards, I networked with people I knew and I attended various networking functions to meet new prospects. With all this preparation, I thought it would be easy to get a new client. Boy was I wrong!

After several weeks without a single call I became discouraged. I lost confidence and wondered what I was doing wrong. I began to doubt if I could really make this business work.

Soon after, I decided to target my marketing within the niche of 'business coaches'. I realize now I should have been even more specific about what kind of business coach I wanted to market to, as it would have made my marketing even that much easier. Why did I choose business coaches as my target market? Over time, I came to realize I enjoyed helping my clients implement online technology to automate and simplify multiple areas of their business. This was the primary concern faced by business coaches and I had become very skilled in helping my clients overcome this challenge. I eliminated other services I had previously offered, changed the language on my marketing material and focused my energy on increasing my position as the 'go to person' for business coaches. It didn't take long for my business to grow even more rapidly as a result of this specialization.

Below are samples of professions many Virtual Assistants have selected as their target markets. This list can but split further into additional, more specific categories.

- Coaches and Consultants
- Professional Speakers
- Authors

- Real Estate Agents
- Attorneys
- Media Relations/Publicists
- Event Planners
- Financial Advisors
- Contractors
- Public Relations Professionals
- Entrepreneurs
- Human Resources Professionals

Let's take a look at some specific questions that can help identify your target market:

- **What kind of work do you enjoy?** Do you enjoy using online technology and implementing automation? Or do you prefer providing more creative type support such as design work? Or maybe you enjoy event or project management type of roles.

- **Who do you enjoy working with?** Do you prefer working with men or women? What age group? What profession?

- **Which past role/job did you enjoy the most and why?** If you previously enjoyed working with a specific profession, perhaps you can transfer your understanding and expertise to your VA business.

- **What does your 'ideal client' look like?** Is your ideal client a well-known professional who makes seven figures? Do they have a family and therefore understand your lifestyle if you also have a family? Are they appreciative of you and what you bring to the table? Do they offer flexibility?

- **Which industry are they in?** It's important to have an interest and personal connection with the type of business you support. Are there any industries that you have absolutely no interest in? For example, for me, I have no interest in the financial industry and would not be interested in working with financial planners.

- **Where are they located?** Because of technology, Virtual Assistants can work with anyone, anywhere. However, voice communication between a client and VA can be challenging depending on the time zone difference. I typically work with people within North America. Because of my schedule (and since I'm in the Pacific Time Zone), it's difficult for me to communicate with someone based in Australia or Europe. You decide what works best for you.

- **How long have they been in business?** Are you interested in working with new business owners who are in 'start-up'? Or do you prefer working with someone who's established and well known in their industry? This may also depend on your level of expertise.

- **How old are they?** Do you have a preference for your client's age group? Do you want to work with someone who is about the same age as you or someone who is older? Younger?

- **Are they male or female?** Are you comfortable working with members of the same or opposite sex? Are there qualities of one or the other that you connect with better?

- **What challenges do they face?** This is important when it comes to marketing yourself to your target market (note: we will cover this in more detail in a later chapter). If you understand the challenges faced by your target market, then you can determine if you have the skills and expertise to work with them. Knowing what obstacles your potential clients face will help you determine if you really should focus on that market or not.

- **What knowledge/expertise do these clients want and need?** Do you have what it takes to help these clients build their business? Can you get training if you don't have the expertise? If you are interested in a specific target market, but lack the knowledge and expertise they need, it may not be a good idea to focus on them until your skills match their needs.

- **What benefits do they want?** What does your target market want from you? Do they typically want you to come in to the office on a weekly basis? Do they want to be able to meet you in person? Is that something you are interested in considering?

- **Who else currently services this market?** I believe there is so much work available that competition is not really a concern at this time, however you need to determine if there is room for you in this market. What do your competitors offer? Can you offer the same or better service? What would make you stand apart from your competitors?

- **Is this market familiar with VAs and how they work?** If your market is not familiar with the VA industry you may find yourself spending a lot of time educating them of the benefits and features you offer. If you're trying to get your business up and running while generating revenue, it may not be in your best interest to select a target market that is unfamiliar with the VA industry. Choose one that is, then come back and help educate later -- once you already have clients and are making money!

- **Can they afford your VA rates?** VA stands for 'Virtual Assistant', not 'Volunteer Assistant'. If your target market can't (or isn't willing to) pay the rates you're charging, then you may need to seriously consider finding another target market. You need to find and work with clients who value your expertise and are willing to pay for that service.

- **How much revenue does their business generate?** If you know your target markets' business generates a certain level of revenue, then you can get a good idea of whether or not they can afford to pay for your services. It also helps to know whether your clients would come to you requiring ongoing support or 'as needed' support.

- **Who do they provide services to?** Who is your markets' target market? Do they target people you are also comfortable with working with? Are you comfortable with their beliefs? Are you passionate about them?

By answering these questions you will start to narrow the kind of professional you want to market your business to.

This is the first critical step in choosing your target market and building your practice.

Over the years, I have spoken to several VAs who have also indicated that once they decided to choose a specific target market, it became much easier for them to identify strategies to help connect, and eventually work with, these professionals.

Let's consider the alternative. Let's say you choose to not select a target market. Your marketing material – website, business cards, yellow pages, advertising ads, brochure and verbal description are designed to include general details on the services you offer. So, as a potential client scans your details, they see what you offer. If it looks the same as other competitors of yours, why would they choose your services over the others? To stand out, you need to speak their language. Doing so lets them know that you 'get' who they are and what they do.

Exercise

Answer the questions below to help you determine your target market:

1. **What kind of work do you enjoy?** (i.e. transcription, writing, online marketing, web design…)

2. **Who do you enjoy working with?** (Women, men, over 50, under 50, fast-paced individuals, slower-paced businesses…)

3. **Which industry / professions are you interested in working with?** (Attorneys, financial planners, realtors…)

4. **What does your ideal client look like?** (Small business owner, business executive, size of business, new or established…)

5. Where are they located? (Your city, state, province, country, international)

6. How long have they been in business? (Under 2 years, over 5 years…)

7. What are their challenges (in their words)? (They don't understand online technology, they can't keep their contacts organized, they want to create online products…)

8. What knowledge/expertise do these clients want and need? (An automated way to keep in touch with their contacts, a database program to house all contact details, a shopping cart system to allow people to purchase items from their website…)

9. What benefits do they want? (Someone with experience using their technology, someone who understands their business model…)

10. What is their preferred method of receiving communication? (TV, radio, yellow pages, Internet…)

11. Who else currently services this market? (i.e. Who are your competitors?)

12. Is this market familiar with VAs and how they work?

13. Can they afford your VA rates?

14. Are you passionate about this market? Does their work excite you?

Now, based on all the information you included above, create a statement to describe your target market.

For example:

I want to work with male business coaches who are between the age of 35 and 45, live in the United States, who are well respected, considered as experts in their market and are earning over $200,000/year.

CHAPTER TWO

On Target - How to Hit a "Bullseye" With Your Target Market (every time)

Once you determine your target market, it is absolutely critical to learn more about them. You'd be surprised how many Virtual Assistants skip this step.

Having spoken with hundreds of small business owners over the years, one of the most common reasons why potential clients hesitate to hire VAs is because they don't feel the VA understands them or their business.

Let's explore what this means a little further.

In order for a potential client to feel confident in exploring the possibility of working with you, they need to feel that you know enough about them and their business so you can appropriately take care of tasks on their behalf. They also want to know what's in it for them – what do you offer that will specifically benefit them and their business.

For example, if you speak with a financial planner about how you can help them, yet have no idea what they do, what they need and what you can do to support them, you will not give them any reason to explore working with you. Your lack of understanding their business will, in most cases, be an immediate "turn-off". Think of it this way -- would you hire a babysitter who knew absolutely nothing about children? Of course not. So, would you expect a financial planner to want to work with you if you didn't know anything about their profession? Of course not.

If your potential client doesn't feel confident that you understand them or their business, they will most likely not become your client.

UNDERSTANDING YOUR TARGET MARKET

In order to understand your target market, you need to learn as much as possible about them. This includes being familiar with:

- What they want to accomplish in their business.
- How they help their clients.
- Education and training they have (or are required to have).
- Organizations/associations they belong to and participate in.
- Common places they visit online.
- Common events they visit offline.
- Publications and trade journals they read and subscribe to online and offline.
- Who the leaders are in their industry.

By reading what they're reading, participating in events they participate in and by learning what they're learning you become familiar with your target markets':
- Interests.
- Common challenges.
- Resources.
- Industry leaders.
- Language – the common terms used in their industry.
- Ongoing trends.

You are now in a much better position to learn even more about your target market.

So, how do you continue gaining an understanding of your target market, on an ongoing basis?

Easy:

- Read their websites to learn how they help their clients.
- Read their articles (online article banks, ezines etc.).
- Do a Google search – what sites are they linked to and have information posted on?
- Subscribe to newsletters/ezines of the places they visit online.
- Subscribe to online groups and participate as appropriate.
- Research their competitors – who else is out there offering the same services/products?

By completing these steps and gaining this knowledge, you have increased your opportunities to connect with potential new clients within your target market. By investing time in this step alone, you put yourself ahead of your competition because now you know: what your client knows, how you can reach them, what challenges they face and, perhaps most importantly, how you can help them overcome these challenges.

When you invest time to research your target market, you can then adjust your marketing language to demonstrate that you understand their challenges and how your offerings are a potential solution to those challenges. When you speak to members of your target market, either by phone or in person, and communicate the solutions you provide to their most common problems, you will capture their interest and most likely be in a better position to build a relationship with them.

If you have not done this in your business already, I challenge you to give it a try.

Remember, you only get one first impression. Make the most of it by demonstrating your understanding of your target market.

Exercise

Questions to Help You Understand Your Target Market

What are the common goals of your target market?

How does your target market help their clients?

What education and/or training does your target market typically have?

What organizations or associations does your target market partici-pate in?

What websites does your target market visit online?

What events does your target market typically attend?

What is your target market reading? Publications, trade journals, books etc. (online and offline)

Who are some of the leaders in their industry?

What are some of the common challenges faced by your target market?

What are the common trends of this market?

Which terms, topics and phrases does your target market use that you should become familiar with?

How can you address their challenges?

RESEARCHING YOUR TARGET MARKET
Use the checklist below to help you learn more about your target market and the challenges they face.

❑ Online newsletters, ezines etc. your target market subscribes to:
-
-
-

❑ Online groups your target market subscribes and participates in:
-
-
-

❑ Websites of key members of this target market:
-
-
-

❑ How do they help their clients?
-
-
-

❑ Key topics of the target market (search for articles etc.):
-
-
-

❑ Competitors and services/products offered:

-
-
-

❑ Magazines/publications read by this target market:

-
-
-

❑ Associations/organizations this target market joins:

-
-
-

UNDERSTANDING YOUR POTENTIAL CLIENT

Wondering why you're not getting hired?

Over the years, in my discussions and work with hundreds of business owners, I've discovered very specific obstacles that prevent business owners from hiring VAs.

Here are some reasons why clients may not be hiring you:

- **You haven't proven you understand their business.** It's critical to demonstrate you understand the challenges your clients face. What keeps them up at night? What stresses them? One of the most common complaints we receive from clients looking for a VA is that the client doesn't feel like the VA understands them, or their business.

- **You haven't proven you understand what they want to ac-complish with their business.** When a client shares their goals, they're looking for you to provide feedback on how you can help them accomplish those goals.

- **You haven't demonstrated your skills or expertise.** In many cases Virtual Assistants focus on the features of working with a VA such as: you work out of your own office so the client won't be required to purchase additional equipment etc. You must demonstrate that you have the skills and expertise to support them in achieving their goals – focus on the benefits you offer that will benefit them.

- **They're not ready: they are not clear on their own goals and priorities.** "Make more money" is a common goal I hear from potential clients. If a client can't tell you how they want to make more money or what they want to accomplish with the next six months, they're likely not quite ready to hire you as their VA. In order for you to be able to best support them, they need to know what their goals are.

- **You haven't demonstrated that you can 'speak their lan-guage'.** Clients want to hire a VA who already understands as much as possible about their business – they don't want to spend time training. Be familiar with common terms or phrases used within their industry and demonstrate that you have taken the time to learn this.

- **You haven't established a relationship (they may not know, like or trust you yet).** Would you invite a stranger into your business operations? Likely not. Developing relationships is critical to building your VA business. Find ways to keep in touch and create a bond so your potential clients will get to know, like and trust you.

- **You haven't proven you understand their challenges or their 'pain'.** This is critical. Understanding where your client really needs help is essential. It may be their specific challenges or it may be challenges faced by the profession as a whole. For example, a common challenge I find within the coaching community is that coaches want to create online products and want to completely automate the purchase process. Their 'pain' is in the setting up of the technology that's required to accomplish this. By understanding and sharing this with them, you put yourself way ahead of other VAs who may be competing for the same clients.

- **You haven't demonstrated you provide solutions to their challenges.** TELL them. Provide an example of the various steps you could implement to solve one of their challenges. In the item above we talked about automating the purchase process for online products. In this case, you could share with your client that they need a shopping cart system and payment gateway in order to accept payments …again, TELL them.

- **They don't think they can afford you.** Clients need to feel the value before they will feel they can afford you. Even if your potential client is a multi-millionaire, if they don't feel the value that you offer, they will feel they can't (or don't want to) afford you. By sharing how you can eliminate the stress and contribute to the growth of their business, they will see the value and find a way to afford you.

- **They don't see the value in your and your services.** If you share how your expertise will impact their business in a positive way, they will see the value. Speak specifically to them and their needs, relating to what they have told you or what you have seen on their website.

- **They're still in the 'education' stage about how to work with a VA.** Professionals who are new to the concept of working 'Virtually' may be reluctant to try using a 'Virtual' Assistant at first. If you feel they may be open to the idea but are reluctant, you can offer to start with a small, one-time project at first. This will help them build confidence in you and your service.

- **You haven't proven to them your value is worth your rate (i.e. you haven't proven to them that you are a good return on their investment – as opposed to being an expense).** If your rates are higher than your competitors, they may not understand why. Also, if you have not demonstrated how your expertise directly relates to the frustrations and challenges their facing, they will not feel your contribution will make a difference to their business. You must communicate this to them in order for them to fully understand.

- **They think they can do it all themselves – they haven't realized the value of delegating the tasks they are not proficient in.** Again, they don't see the value of you or your expertise. Beware of clients who feel they're better off taking care of the tasks on their own. They may ask for your assistance only when they're stuck and feeling at their highest level of frustration. They may not be the ideal client.

- **They 'don't know what they don't know'.** These clients may be in the 'education stage' where they're still unfamiliar with how a VA can really help them. If you feel they have great potential then you may guide them a little by taking inventory (covered in a later chapter) and by explaining how you can help. However, if they can't tell you their goals or priorities, they are not ready to work with you.

- **You took too long to respond to their inquiry.** Responding in a timely manner is critical. Remember, they want to experience your professionalism before they even consider having you work with them. Make sure to make a good first impression.

Let's discover how you can eliminate these obstacles and make room for clients to hire you.

Every profession has common challenges. By understanding the challenges or *pain* faced by your market, you'll be able to identify exactly what services and solutions to offer to them to help eliminate that pain.

When you clearly communicate with your prospects your awareness of their pain and you can suggest solutions that addresses that pain, you will spark their interest. They will feel understood and they will see value in hiring you.

WHAT ARE THEIR CHALLENGES?

Maybe your client needs help with sales. Or maybe they need help organizing their client records. Maybe their challenge is in the area of marketing their own services.

Whatever the challenge they face, the services and solutions you offer should be in direct alignment with tackling those challenges.

The chart below includes examples of challenges faced by the coaching profession and sample solutions VAs can provide:

Challenge faced by potential client	Sample solution offered by VA
I want to sell my digital products on my website and completely automate the delivery.	Shopping cart/merchant account expertise, knowledge of digital delivery options.
I want to add an ezine sign up form on my website.	Expertise in using broadcast/ezine delivery programs to format/deliver ezine and create sign up to be added to website.
I want to offer a free teleseminar to my database.	Knowledge of specific steps to setting up a teleseminar including bridge line, audio recording software, helping with broadcasting correspondence to database.
I want to generate more traffic to my website.	Knowledge of general list building activities and understanding technology required to have the traffic contribute to a database for your client.

By defining your target market, understanding what they do, understanding their challenges and demonstrating your solutions, you are significantly increasing your chances of connecting with potential clients, peaking their interest in you, building a relationship and potentially adding them to your own client base.

My Story...

A few months after starting my business, I decided to focus on realtors as my target market. Even in my small city, there were thousands of realtors. I thought it was a sure thing that I would line up even a few of them as long-term clients. I found a listing of all the realtors in my local area, confirmed the top sellers and emailed them to introduce myself.

With over 300,000 realtors in the region, you'd think it would be easy to find a few regular clients, right? Wrong.

I received only a few responses to my emails. Still, I was determined to make this work so picked up the phone and followed up with people who had not responded to my email introduction. This was way out of my comfort zone, but I forced myself to make the calls anyway.

I stepped further out of my comfort zone when I asked various real estate agencies to allow me to come in and introduce myself and speak to the realtors about how I could assist them.

Many realtors were too busy to speak with me. Others kindly made the time and asked me various questions about how I could support them. I hadn't done my homework. I confidently spoke about the services and expertise I offered, yet I barely touched on the solutions I offered to overcome their challenges. In fact, I had very little understanding of the challenges these realtors faced or how I could provide a solution to them. Most of my presentation focused on the features of the VA industry.

I bombed for various reasons:

- I was not familiar with the challenges of this market.
- I did not appropriately communicate solutions I could offer to overcome these challenges.
- I was not aware of the technology or language they used within their profession.
- They were not familiar with the VA profession and were skeptical.
- They were unwilling to pay a typical VA rate.
- I was not excited about this work and therefore was not interested in learning about the challenges they faced.
- I was desperate for clients and this was most likely reflected in my discussion.

I learned a lot from this experience. I learned I needed to find, understand, be excited about and educate myself about my target market. It was time to determine the type of client I wanted to work with and invest the time to learn more about them.

CHECKLIST:

Will your prospect hire you?

Have you:
- ☐ Proven that you understand what they want to accomplish with their business?
- ☐ Demonstrated your skills and expertise?
- ☐ Demonstrated that you can 'speak their language'?
- ☐ Established a relationship with them? (do they know, like or trust you?).
- ☐ Proven an understanding of their pain and offered a solution?
- ☐ Proven to them that your value is worth your rate (or that you are a good return on their investment as opposed to being an expense)?

Do they:
- ☐ Have the means to afford you?
- ☐ Know enough about how to work with a VA?
- ☐ Know what their own goals and priorities are?
- ☐ Think they can do it all themselves?
- ☐ Need help with understanding the value of delegating the tasks they are not proficient in?

FEATURES VS. BENEFITS

A common mistake made by Virtual Assistants is focusing on the *features* of the VA industry rather than the benefits offered to help their chosen target market.

A *feature* is an item that is offered by everyone within the Virtual Assistant community. We all work virtually and therefore we offer the same features based on our profession.

A *benefit* is what the client will experience from working with you in relation to their specific needs and challenges. This is what makes you unique and sets you apart from your competition.

The Virtual Assistant industry is still relatively new and often when VAs are asked what they do for a living, they respond by highlighting general features of the industry.

Features of the VA industry include:

- We are available when you need us.
- We work from our fully-equipped home office.
- Charging expenses for only time and materials related to your project.
- No extra equipment or office costs for your business.
- No employee related taxes, benefits packages, insurance to pay, vacations or losing valuable hours due to sick time.

These features are general statements and do not specifically identify how you would be the best VA to work with. In order to capture the attention and interest of a potential client, you need to identify and tell them how you will help solve their specific challenges.

While it's important to note these VA features to help educate professionals about our industry, when trying to attract clients, it may not be enough to spark their interest. They want to hear the answer to the question, "What's in it for me?" How will your business provide a direct solution to them? In other words, what is the benefit you offer.

Communicating the benefits you offer can mean the difference between getting a client, and not getting a client.

Consider the following two statements -

"Working with me means you don't have to purchase additional equipment or make room for me in your office." *This is a feature statement.*

Vs.

"I can help you develop a system to ensure you keep in touch with your own prospects on a regular basis and therefore convert them into paying customers and generate more revenue." – *This is an "I am the solution" statement.*

Which statement do you think will capture the attention of your potential client?

The first statement includes a feature of the VA industry. This is certainly an attractive and valid point to share with potential clients, however it is generic and does not relate specifically to a challenge the client is facing. Plus, this is most likely a feature many other Virtual Assistants have or will use when speaking with potential clients.

Be clear about what is in it for them, the client.

The second statement tells the prospect how you can solve the challenge they are experiencing, and how it will help them build their own business. If your potential clients understand that you will contribute to their business and they are receiving a return on their investment in you, they will be much more likely to sign up to work with you.

Understanding Challenge + Providing Solution = More Clients

It's a simple formula, but by learning about the challenges your target market faces, you can position yourself with the expertise needed to solve this problem and communicate this to them. If you don't already have this expertise, you can seek out resources to learn more.

Do you speak their language?

Every profession has jargon: specific terms, phrases and topics that often have little meaning outside their profession. When it comes to fully understanding and specializing in working with a target market, it's critical to become familiar with their 'language'.

There are many benefits to understanding their language, it:

- Demonstrates your knowledge when you speak with potential clients.
- Proves your interest and understanding of their challenges.
- Allows you to identify the specific services you can offer that your market needs and wants from you.
- Increases your reputation and professionalism.
- Significantly increases their interest and confidence in working with you.
- Gives you an added advantage over your competitors.

All things being equal, if a prospect is considering hiring you vs. your competitor, the VA who understands their language will definitely have the advantage.

My Story...

When I first chose my target market, I was unfamiliar with many of their common terms. I had never heard of such things as: 'bridge lines', 'mini course', 'autoresponders', 'shopping cart', 'teleclass' and 'prep form', for example. But I made it a priority to learn what they meant and how they impacted my clients.

Once I did learn the jargon of my market, I was able to demonstrate my understanding and respond appropriately. This contributed to my success in having a natural conversation and eventually finding and retaining clients.

IN ACTION:

In the Multiple Streams Team, we help online-based business owners (mainly coaches) automate and build their businesses. In my role, I am fortunate to speak with at least four new potential clients every week. I learn about their business, what they want to accomplish and educate them as to how a VA can support them. I then match the potential client with a VA sub-contractor on our team. Our entire team prides ourselves in speaking the "MSOCI" – the Multiple Streams of Coaching Income - language. MSOCI is a business blueprint, with dozens of proven ways to package coaching within a business. Many of our clients follow this business plan and benefit greatly from working with a VA who also understands this model.

(Visit **www.msoci.com** to get your own copy of this fabulous book, written by Andrea J. Lee)

Two of the common terms used in the MSOCI model include 'Pink Spoon' and 'One Banana' websites.

A Pink Spoon is simply a single, compelling and free offer provided on a website in exchange for the contact details of website visitors. Think of the ice cream shop – you get a sample of ice cream on a Pink Spoon before deciding to make a purchase. With a website, this Pink Spoon offer often comes in the form of a mini ecourse, report or audio recording. Website visitors can obtain this report simply by entering their name and email address on the website form which is linked to a program, such as your shopping cart, to automate the delivery of your Pink Spoon. By offering the Pink Spoon, website visitors are provided with free, valuable information in exchange for their contact details.

For example, at **www.MultipleStreamsTeam.com,** we offer a free ecourse and a, "101 Ways to Use a VA" report. This is our Pink Spoon – we offer it at no charge in exchange for the name and email address of our website visitors.

Another example is an ecourse for VA's called, "The 10 Critical Skills for a Thriving Virtual Assistant Practice." If you haven't already subscribed to this ecourse, I strongly encourage you to do so. You can find it at: **www.GrowYourVABiz.com.**

A 'One Banana' website is a simple, one page website that includes one main call to action. For example, **www.HotSkillsVATraining.com** is a One Banana website. It includes a variety of information, all pertaining to the Hot Skills VA Training program. The call to action is registering for the program.

When I speak with a potential client who tells me they need help with setting up their Pink Spoon, the Multiple Streams Team knows exactly what they're looking for and we know exactly what questions to ask them.

The benefit to the client is:

- They don't need to take the time to educate the VA on what 'Pink Spoon' means and why they want to have one on their website.
- They don't have to learn about the software needed to implement their Pink Spoon - they know that we understand exactly what they're looking for.

This gives the potential client confidence in our abilities - they trust us and want to build a relationship with us.

Understanding the common language of your target market is just one more easy, yet incredible way to demonstrate you are a VA worth working with.

WHAT SERVICES TO OFFER

Assuming you have selected and researched your target market, based on the previous chapters, you now know:

- How they help their own clients.
- What they read.
- What their challenges are (and what pain they are experiencing).
- What terms and phrases they use.
- What topics they are interested in addressing.

Now that you have these details, you can appropriately identify the best services to offer your target market.

Virtual Assistants around the world offer a wide range of professional administration services.

These may include:

- Word processing
- Event planning
- Newsletters/ezines
- Spreadsheet development
- Online research
- PowerPoint presentations
- Graphic Design

- Scheduling
- Contact/database management
- Desktop publishing
- Transcription
- Website design/maintenance
- Proofreading
- Mail Merging

Take a second to review the list one more time. Consider your potential client as they:

- Review a list of these services on your website.
- Have an in-person discussion with you about the above services you offer.

Now take a moment to consider whether these services will attract or create enough incentive for your prospects to contact you.

If you are sharing with a prospect the services you provide, it needs to be phrased in a way that directly relates to your target markets' challenges instead of to the general public. All VAs have these kinds of services listed on their website, so what makes you stand out?

At the beginning of the book, we discussed the importance of selecting a target market. It gives us a better opportunity to fully understand and connect with potential clients in a specific market, rather than trying to understand and build exposure with numerous markets.

By selecting services that are specific to your target market, you are identifying even more with who you want to work with and how you can help them.

Here is a list of common services and skills many business owners are looking for in a VA:

Setting up, customizing and managing the shopping cart.	Creating and Using Autoresponders.
Setting up the 'buy button' on a website – to include taxes, shipping, digital delivery, etc.	Formatting and distributing broadcasts with tracking and statistical components.
Setting up teleclass registration.	Blog Posting and Maintenance.
Website Editing and Maintenance.	Handling Customer Service.
Assisting with Product Development.	Assisting with Traffic and List Building activities.

You may find, over time that you want to narrow your focus and services even more and specialize in just a few key areas that are critical to your target market (and that you enjoy).

By specializing your services and demonstrating your expertise in these areas, you will become a known and sought-after expert within your target market. This doesn't mean you limit your services to just one or two items and do nothing more. It means that you specialize in a specific area that will peak the interest of your potential client.

By the way, building credibility as a specialized expert also means you can increase your rates.

SPECIALIZING YOUR SERVICES

If you know your target market struggles with keeping in continuous communication with their database subscribers, what kind of solution can you provide them?

If you tell them you can help with managing their database, they may be interested, but not completely ready to pull out their credit card.

However, if you tell them you specialize in helping members of your target market manage their database and keep in touch with their subscribers by assisting them with creating a schedule for regular communication - such as a monthly ezine, follow up emails, announcements etc. – they will be more intrigued and more likely to pull out their credit card and sign up to work with you. In fact, they may be willing to pay more than a typical VA rate because you have communicated your expertise in a way that will specifically give them the results they want.

If you can communicate the benefits your potential clients will receive from working with you and the value they will experience and therefore the results they will experience, you will be well you on your way to building a long-term relationship with a client.

Communicate the Benefits +

Understand the Value +

Experience the Results =

Long-term client relationship

My Story...

I discovered the benefits of specializing my skills a few years ago. The business coaches I worked with were often challenged with spending too much time manually completing day-to-day business related tasks. I discovered that by incorporating just one piece of online technology into their business, they would save multiple hours each week – time they could spend in marketing and building their business, or generating revenue.

I started by identifying areas I recognized they could be more efficient in. After identifying the problem, I became very familiar with the online programs that would offer a solution by automating and creating a more seamless process.

I soon became known and respected among business coaches as the 'go to' person when it came to spotting inefficiencies and offering solutions. I offered many other services to my clients, but by specializing in this area, my market could immediately identify me as the VA who stood apart from my competitors.

WHAT WILL THEY PAY FOR?

Another detail to consider when it comes to learning about your target market and what services to offer is what they are willing to pay for.

Clients will pay for solution-based support. They will not pay for general-based support.

Solution-based support is where you identify a specific challenge and offer a specific solution to this challenge. For example, if your client needs help setting up products for sale on their website, your expertise with a shopping cart program, autoresponders and automating the entire purchase process is solution-based support.

General-based support describes the general type services, such as word processing, spreadsheets and data entry. General-based support does not clearly illustrate how your services contribute to solving a challenge faced by your target market.

Virtual Assistant rates range anywhere from $25 to $50 per hour. According to the VANetworking.com Survey, over 30% of VAs charge between $30-$40 per hour (Visit http://www.vanetworking.com/ survey/ for additional details.). By offering solution-based services and specializing in a few areas, you will be able to bill your services at a higher rate than if you were simply offering general services. If you have proven yourself to be an expert in a specific niche, your clients will know they will receive a better return on their investment and have no trouble with paying your higher rate.

Start by doing some research. What do other VAs charge for similar services? What will your clients likely pay for support in this area?

Once you determine the rate you will charge, be sure that you can (and will) provide that level of support. For example, if your hourly rate is at the higher end of the range for a typical VA, say, $50/hour – you need to provide $50/hour worth of value (you won't get away with offering only $25/hour of value). A client that receives the level of assistance they are expecting at the higher rate will never question the amount. Instead, they will see your contribution to their business as an investment rather than a monthly expense.

Target Market + Specialization = More $$

BE A PROFIT CENTER

When I refer to Virtual Assistants as being a *profit center*, I'm refer-ring to how the VA contributes to the growth of the business. For example, is the VA taking care of tasks that will generate revenue or contribute to generating revenue? If a VA is performing basic administrative tasks and waiting to be delegated to, they are not considered a profit center.

There are times in every business when you may question how you are spending your money. Your clients are no different.

We will dig a little deeper into this subject in a later chapter, how-ever I would like you to consider what you can do to have potential and current clients see you as a profit center for their business.

Exercise:

What are the challenges/pain faced by your target market?

Why do they experience these challenges? (do they lack the skill, money, time?)

What are some common terms used by your target market?

Based on your skills and expertise, what solutions can you provide?

What do these terms mean?

How can you prove you understand these terms?

How can you specialize?

How much is your target market willing to pay for this support?

How can you be seen as a 'profit center' by your potential and current clients?

CHAPTER THREE

Brand 'You'

Once you have determined your target market and learned about their challenges you are ready to create a buzz so they know you exist. Building your presence and marketing yourself can be challenging. You will be consumed with completing tasks for your clients and will find yourself out of time to market and build your own business.

One of the biggest mistakes I've seen VAs make is not marketing their business once they have secured a few clients. Marketing yourself and building relationships with your target market should not stop, even when your business is full.

One of my favorite quotes about this was written by my client, Stephen Fairley, "Marketing is an ongoing process, not an event." You must always be marketing your business. Don't wait until you need more clients or more revenue to start marketing.

There are literally thousands of ways to build your business within your target market. We are going to uncover a few.

MARKETING ONLINE

Marketing online is the most cost effective way to promote your business. By leveraging technology and the Internet, you can easily get your name out there and build relationships with people from around the world. Because of the nature of the VA profession, this works to your advantage as you can work with anyone no matter where they are located.

Let's talk about a few ways you can build your online presence:

A Professional Website/Blog

According to a survey, given by **www.VANetworking.com** in October 2007, 85% of Virtual Assistants have a website.

(*Source: Virtual Assistant Networking Association (VANA) The Media Virtual Assistant Survey. The Largest Global Meeting Place Online for Aspiring and Successful Virtual Assistants).

Virtual Assistants don't need an extravagant website, but they do need a professional one that speaks to their target market and appropriately demonstrates the expertise they offer.

Websites copy is critical. When a professional comes to your website, you want to easily identify that you offer the solutions to their challenges. Many VAs have a traditional website that is equivalent to an online brochure – one that includes details about "services, about us, rates, testimonials" etc. These details are helpful to incorporate in website copy, but remember, when a prospect visits your website, they want to know 'what's in it for them' -- what do you offer that specifically relates to their challenges.

Another critical component to your website is your Pink Spoon. Your Pink Spoon is the free item – the main call to action – that you offer to your website visitors in exchange for their contact details (name and email). By collecting the contact details of your website visitors, you create an opportunity to keep in touch with them and build a relationship. When you have an opening in your business for additional clients, you now have a list of potential prospects you can email and advise them you have availability.

When writing copy for your website, consider the keywords your prospects may search for and include them throughout the copy and meta tags -- information such as keywords and descriptions of a webpage that is stored in the head of an HTML document. For more information on how to optimize your website for search engines, review current search engine optimization strategies available on the Internet. The use of keywords, meta tags and search engine optimization strategies is geared towards improving the volume and quality of traffic to your website.

Keep your website up-to-date. If you don't already have a blog – get one! Blogs are inexpensive and very easy to update. Sign up at **www.typepad.com** for free to get your blog started. Once you have your blog, post regularly -- at least 3-4 times a week.

Article Submission

Writing and submitting articles is one of the best and most cost effective ways to get your name and website out on the Internet. By posting your articles to various article banks - such as **www.articlecity.com, www.articlehub.com** and **www.amazines.com,** your articles will get picked up by other websites and, over time, your name and website will appear all over the Internet. When a prospect searches for a topic covered in your article, they will be able to read your content and visit your website to learn more about you and your business.

Here are a few things to consider when writing your articles:
- Write your article specific for your target market. Make sure it offers quality content and isn't too general.
- Grab their attention with a great title.
- Use bullet points to demonstrate key points. This also makes the article easier to read.

- Use the article to educate your target market about a specific topic, rather than focusing on telling them about your services.
- Be sure to include a byline (your shortened bio) at the bottom of your article with an incentive to encourage them to click the link to your website. For example:

Cindy Greenway, a Virtual Assistant since 2003, works with reputable clients in the coaching profession. *To learn how a Virtual Assistant can help you build your business, visit* *www.multiplestreamsteam.com* *and sign up for the free "Boost Business with a VA" Report. Virtual Assistants can learn more about the skills they need to have, as well as how to build and sustain a profitable VA business by visiting www.growyourvabiz.com and requesting the free '10 Critical Skills' ecourse.*

Press Releases

Business owners often shy away from press releases because they think they don't know how to write one. However, writing and distributing press releases is a great way to build an online presence.

Write a press release about something newsworthy in your business and post it to various press release submission sites, such as **www.prweb.com** or **www.businesswire.com.** Newsworthy items may include a new product you have available, a mention of an award presented to you, an announcement about an upcoming event etc.

Just like articles, you will find your press release posted to various places online. Visit **www.prweb.com** for sample press releases and details on how to submit your press release.

Joint Venture Partners

Building joint ventures – a win/win relationship with another professional who offers a service or product that complements what you offer – is a fantastic way to build your business and gain exposure to additional people in your target market. This can be very simple. For example, if your potential joint venture partner and you each have an ezine, ask them if they would consider including one of your articles in their ezine and offer to do the same in return.

One of the great benefits of joint ventures is you get a chance to put your name in front of a completely new audience of people who may not know you. If these prospects already know, like and trust your joint venture partner, they are more likely to pay attention to your information and click on the link to your website. This option is cost-effective – usually there is no exchange of fees with a simple partnership like this.

Referral Sources

Aligning yourself with professionals who share the same target market as you can prove to be invaluable.

By creating this network of professionals, each of you can recommend and refer your services to others who may need it.

As a Virtual Assistant you may want to consider building relationships with others who service your target market, including: Web designers, Bookkeepers, Accountants, Copywriters, Search Engine Optimization Experts, Marketing Coaches, Graphic Designers.

When you or a client needs these services, you can refer to your referral network and recommend an expert for your client – and members of your referral network will do the same for you.

In the Multiple Streams Team, we have relationships with various professionals with different areas of expertise. When someone needs a logo created, we call on the Graphic Designer in our referral network to help with the project. When she connects with someone in need of online support, she refers them to us.

Join Discussion Lists

This method can be time consuming and not provide immediate noticeable results however, if you participate on a regular basis, you will find yourself building relationships with other group members and also building your credibility.

Thousands of online discussion groups can be found at **www.yahoo.com** and **www.msn.com.** Do a search on groups that fit your target market and the services you provide. For example, if you help Financial Planners find new clients, then use appropriate search terms to find the best groups. If your target market is Business Coaches and you help them create new products, then you would use different search terms to locate the best groups to join.

When you join a discussion list, you can choose to either have the new posts sent to you via email, or you log into the group and view the new posts. By having the new messages sent to you via email, you will be able to review and respond to posts quickly therefore creating a presence and building credibility with group members.

As you read new posts submitted by other members, make note of the challenges they are expressing as well as how you can contribute. Be very careful when responding to posts as most discussion groups do not allow self-promotion. Your response should directly relate to the question and offer value.

Here are a few tips to consider when participating in online discussion lists:

- Research and join a few discussion lists for your target market. If you join too many, you will be flooded with new emails (depending on how active the group is).
- When you see a topic you can respond to, do so ASAP. And remember, your response will be viewed by everyone in the group.
- Include a good signature block at the end of every post that includes:
  - Your name.
  - Your business name.
  - Your website URL.
  - A call to action.

This is your only way to 'promote' yourself so include some kind of incentive, such as, "Visit my website www.mywebsite.com to get a free report on the *Top 10 Delegating Mistakes You May Be Making*." This will not only encourage people to click through to your website to learn more about you, it will also give them a chance to sign up for your free report. Another subscriber added to your database!

Here is a sample of a potential signature block for your discussion list posts:

Cindy Greenway, Virtual Manager
Multiple Streams Team
www.MultipleStreamsTeam.com

*Get Your Copy of the "101 Ways to Boost Business With a VA" Report at www.MultipleStreamsTeam.com

*Note how I included a link and a call to action to my website. My hope is that if a discussion list member reads my response and is

interested in what I do, they will have a reason to go to my website and sign up for my Pink Spoon.

Public Speaking

Virtual Assistants are often intimidated by public speaking, however it is an option to consider. It can be an opportunity to build relationships with members of your target market. Depending on your target market and the kind of work they do, you may consider offering a teleseminar or online interview, instead of face-to-face speaking.

When speaking you provide quality information to your target market and it also allows you to demonstrate your understanding and expertise – giving potential clients a way to get to know, like and trust you.

Here are some tips to think about when using public speaking to build your business:

- Research how to best reach your target market: in-person speaking or online speaking?
- Research organizations/associations who will allow you to come in for a short presentation.
- Search online for potential joint ventures or other opportunities to offer 30-60 minute teleclasses to your target market.
- Keep your presentation short, concise and with a call to action so attendees can visit your website and potentially sign up for your database.

Marketing Offline

When we think offline marketing, most of us immediately think of advertising. As a VA, I have paid for advertising only twice. In 2003, I paid for an advertisement in a women's magazine where the feature article was about the coaching profession. In 2004, I paid for a yellow pages ad.

What a waste of money.

I actually did receive numerous calls from the yellow pages ad, however most of them were from 'price shoppers' – people wanting information about my rates or needing help with an urgent project that needed to be done the same afternoon. These calls were not worth the cost of the ad.

To market yourself and your business, you don't need to spend thousands of dollars on an advertising campaign. Since 2004 I have not spent a single penny on advertising. Neither should you.

There is an abundance of business owners looking for a qualified and responsive Virtual Assistant to join their business. By considering the points outlined in this book to help you better understand your target market and also what to communicate to your target market you should have no trouble finding clients to join your business.

Some of the problems Virtual Assistants face with advertising:

- Many professionals are new or unfamiliar with the VA market - they need to be educated before they will simply consider contacting a VA from an advertisement.
- Ads are often too general: not specifically worded, distributed or reached by the specific market – therefore not cost effective.
- Advertising is expensive. Your marketing dollars can be spent in more productive, results-oriented ways.

If your target market consists of online-based business professionals, then you will want to invest in online marketing strategies.

For target markets that are not online based, consider networking by joining an association or organization specific to your target market. When you join these groups, inquire whether you can speak at an upcoming event or meeting to help educate members about the VA industry and how the members could benefit from the services you offer.

Networking

Networking is the opportunity to make new contacts and build relationships with new prospects. Be prepared and make the most of your time when networking with your target market.

Networking can be split into two categories:
1.   In-person networking events
2.   Social networking

1. In-Person Networking

In-person networking can be beneficial if your niche market is located within your local area. A common mistake made by many professionals is attending networking events for members of their own profession. If you are investing time to meet and build relationships with potential clients in your target market, it's important to consider networking at events for those of your target market.

In the next section we focus on how to make the most of the people you meet at networking events.

2. Social Networking

Social Networking has exploded recently on the internet – between Facebook, LinkedIn, MySpace and others, you can connect and build relationships with people all over the world just by creating a profile, finding people you already know and connecting with others to start and build a relationship. (If you have a Facebook profile, I invite you to add me as a friend. Let me know you have read this book!)

Depending on your target market, decide which networking option is best for you. Having a personal, in-person relationship can out-weigh a virtual relationship, however if your target market is based online or in places other than your local area, you may be better off with investing in online type activities.

CRITICAL KEY: KEEP IN TOUCH

How many times have you met a prospect, never to follow-up after the first meeting or to follow-up only a few times and then give up.

According to various studies, it takes an average 8-10 tries to connect with potential clients. This means if you send an email, and leave two voice mail messages, you are completing only a third of what you may need in order to secure a client.

Keeping in touch with your prospects may mean the difference between building relationships and converting prospects into paying clients and being forgotten all together.

It's critical to keep in touch with prospects, but do you? And how many times are you likely to follow-up?

Many of us are uncomfortable and dislike following-up with prospects, however it is an essential ingredient when it comes to building relationships with people we meet who may be potential clients in the future. Even if you feel you have made a good attempt at following up with someone and they have not returned your call or email, persist. Your perseverance will remind your prospect that you are available and interested in working with them.

Think back to a situation where someone called you numerous

times about a solution they offered. Did you call them back right away? Did you respond to their inquiry? Even if you were interested, did you follow-up immediately? In today's world, we receive thousands of messages via the Internet, phone, radio, television etc. It's impossible to do everything we want to do in a day and we often need reminding.

The key is to stay in touch with your prospect in a natural way. Perhaps you have an article you can send them based on a something they had expressed interest in. Or maybe you found a piece of software online that will solve a challenge they told you they were experiencing. By keeping in touch and reminding your prospect you are available to help them and providing some good information you will stand apart from your competition.

In further chapters, we will discuss more on introducing yourself both online and offline.

CHECKLIST:
How will you promote your business?

Online:
- ☐ Article writing and submission.
- ☐ Press Release writing and submission.
- ☐ Online Networking in lists, forums, websites.
- ☐ Website – using keywords and speaking directly to your target market.
- ☐ Pink Spoon – an automated solution to keeping in contact with prospects.
- ☐ Joint Ventures – creating a win/win relationship.
- ☐ Online Search Engine Optimization Marketing.
- ☐ Online Newsletter.

- ☐ Online Banner Advertising.
- ☐ Email Marketing Camp.

Offline:
- ☐ Networking at local groups.
- ☐ Print Advertising – Newspaper/Magazine Ads.
- ☐ Submitting Press Releases to print publications.
- ☐ Submitting articles to print publications.
- ☐ Yellow Pages.
- ☐ Trade Shows.
- ☐ Cold Calls.
- ☐ Media Kits.
- ☐ Flyers/Brochures/Postcards.
- ☐ Business Cards.

My Story...

Because my target market consists of coaches who also run their business online, I decided to stick to marketing myself and my business on the Internet.

One of the big mistakes I made (and I know many Virtual Assistants are making the same mistake) was not having a Pink Spoon.

I've mentioned the Pink Spoon a few times already because it really is a foundational piece of an online business.

When I started meeting potential clients – either by sending them introduction emails, leaving voicemail messages or even when I submitted my own articles online, I was directing them to my website to learn more about me and my business.

I never really knew how many people were visiting my website – I had no way to measure the success of my follow-up.

Had I known about the Pink Spoon at the time, things would have been a lot different.

Think of these two scenarios:

You send people to your website to get more information about yourself, but have no way to capture their contact details (name and email address).

OR

You send people to your website to give them more information about yourself and your business, and you offer them an attractive, free offer that entices them so they are willing to provide you with their name and email address in exchange for your free offer.

Which option best helps both you and the website visitor? By having a Pink Spoon available on your website, you are:

- Offering free information to educate prospects on how you provide solution-based services.
- Collecting contact details for potential clients.
- Building your business platform.
- Staying in contact with your prospects by automating an autoresponder series (a series of emails that are sent to subscribers at specific time intervals).

If you don't have a Pink Spoon on your website, I challenge you to create one immediately. It doesn't need to be a difficult task – write a quick series of emails that provide value to the subscribers on a specific topic they are challenged with that you offer a solution to. For example, at **www.GrowYourVABiz.com**, we offer a *"The 10 Critical Skills for a Thriving Virtual Assistant Practice"* ecourse. It tells subscribers about the skills they must have as VAs, in order to build a successful practice (it based on the many conversations we've had with business owners).

This ecourse provides solid information and allows us to keep in touch with our subscribers on an ongoing basis. Every month we also send out an ezine to this list - another form of providing quality information.

Once your Pink Spoon is set up on your website, tell people about it. If you've met someone at a networking function, tell them, "Check out my website at **www.yoururl.com** and you can sign up to receive (insert your offer here)." Also include info about your Pink Spoon when you submit articles, press releases or any other item online.

CHAPTER FOUR

Let's Do Lunch

Introducing yourself appropriately to your prospects is the difference between a possible working relationship and no relationship at all.

There are several steps to consider when introducing yourself to a new contact. There are several additional factors to consider in order to convert this new contact into a prospect and, ultimately, into a client.

Whether your target market is based online or not will determine how you will reach out and introduce yourself. No matter how you connect with new prospects, there are several keys to ensuring you make a lasting impression and are not forgotten.

KEYS TO INTRODUCING YOURSELF AND BUILDING RELATIONSHIPS:

1. Initial Contact (email or in person) – identify with the challenges and demonstrate your solutions.
2. Research the Individual.
3. Introductory letter.
4. Keep track.
5. Follow up.
6. Be prepared.

1. Initial Contact

When you introduce yourself – either via email or in person – it is critical to connect with the person and identify that you understand their profession and communicate how your services solve specific challenges they face. Remember, what's in it for them?

2. Research the Individual

Before sending an introductory letter or attending or following up from an in-person event, look up your contact's website to learn more about them. By gaining an understanding of what they offer you can tweak your letter to show you have spent time learning about them. Your prospects will recognize your effort in getting to know about them by the details you include in your letter.

3. Introductory Letter

If you will be using email, draft an introductory letter and identify several tasks you know your target market needs assistance with. By addressing their pain and sharing the solutions you offer to help eliminate this pain, you are more likely to gain their interest.

4. Keep track

Use a database program or keep a spreadsheet with details of who you have sent an introductory email to and their contact details (name, website, date you sent the letter etc.). This is an important step and can be as simple as creating an Excel spreadsheet with several columns to hold your details.

When I originally started my business, I created a very simple spreadsheet:

Name	Business Name	URL	Phone #	Email	Where Met	Notes	Follow-up Dates	Follow-up Details

By keeping this data up-to-date, you will have the latest information at your fingertips.

5. Follow-up

By using a system such as the table above, you can easily track your activity and check-in with the prospect if you do not receive a response back within a few days. Decide if you will send a second email or pick up the phone instead and attempt to make a voice connection.

In your attempts to contact your prospect, remember to continue identifying how the solutions you offer will help alleviate the challenges they are experiencing.

Many Virtual Assistants will have already stopped in their contact and follow-up attempts by this point. If you continue and persist, you will be ahead of the majority of other Virtual Assistants who are also trying to secure new clients.

In order to experience more success, be persistent with your follow up strategies until a prospect lets you know they are not interested or if you have already exhausted attempts (more than 8-10 times) to follow up.

By continuing to connect with your prospects, you are providing them with a reminder of who you are. Ultimately, you want them to like you and you want to build a relationship with them. You want them to learn to trust you enough to potentially work with you, or at least refer you to their colleagues who may need your support.

An important tip many business owners have shared with me is the need for VAs to reply quickly with the appropriate information when a prospect contacts you (via phone or email). If it takes you 24 hours to respond to their email – this isn't good enough and may create hesitation in wanting to work with you. This doesn't mean you are on a 24-hour alert to new emails, however you should respond quickly and professionally (no typos!) as soon as possible.

6. Be Prepared

Marketing yourself and your business can be scary. If you're new to the business world you may feel uncomfortable and intimidated by more experienced professionals.

Meeting new contacts in person is often more challenging than meeting them online. In person you have facial expressions, body language, and tone to work with. However with online connections, you need to be cautious with the wording of your emails as the tone or language within emails can be interpreted differently by different people.

With the VA industry being still relatively new, you may experience discomfort and feel unprepared to answer questions asked by your new contacts.

How many times have you responded to the question, "What do you do?" with, "I'm a Virtual Assistant." You most likely felt uncomfortable with the look on the person's face if they had no idea what a Virtual Assistant does.

Virtual Assistants face two challenges when they meet new people in person:

1. The term Virtual Assistant is still largely unrecognized in many circles. Think of this as an opportunity to educate the business community on the benefits, features, results etc. that come with hiring a VA.

2. The business community often views the administrative role as a traditional one that stays within the office – they have trouble understanding how to work with someone 'virtually'. It's difficult for some professionals to consider how work can be done outside of the office, let alone in a different state/province, country or even continent!

To help prepare yourself and build your confidence in meeting new prospects, take time to document questions you have already been asked or ones you think will be asked of you and create a standard response including exactly what you want to communicate to your new contact.

Here are common questions you may be asked by new contacts:

- What do you do?
- What areas do you excel in?
- What are your strengths / weaknesses?
- How have you helped others in my business market?
- What skills do you offer?
- What services do you offer?
- What are your rates?
- Why should I consider working with you?
- Why would I hire you when I can hire someone at a much lower rate?
- How does working virtually really work?
- Do you come to my office?
- How can you specifically help me with my business?

By preparing your responses to these standard questions, you will feel much more comfortable and appear more confident to share details about your profession.

Creating your own introduction:

Many marketing books suggest creating an, 'elevator speech'. An elevator speech is a 10 to 30 second introduction of your business you use when you connect and engage with new contacts. However, these 'speeches' can often sound rehearsed unless you include your own style and language.

As you build your confidence and use your own words to describe who you are and what you do, it will become easier and you will, in most cases, engage in great conversation. By taking the time to learn about your new contact and their challenges by listening carefully to what they tell you, you can customize your response even more so that it is directly related to their circumstance and reflects how you provide a solution.

You have only one chance to make a lasting first impression. By being prepared, you increase your chances of making your first impression a positive one.

Listen to what your new contact is telling you. How can you appropriately include details in your discussion that reflect who you are and how you can help them?

Here's an example of how a Virtual Assistant may respond when asked, "What do you do?"

"I work with online based business coaches and support them in using online technology to automate tasks and also create products to assist them in generating more revenue and building their business."

Create your own response:

I work with _____ and help them solve/develop/
become _____ so they can _____
_____.

Before you attend your next networking or business event, practice
how you will respond to the common questions about who you are
and what you do.

What is your follow-up plan?

How and where will you record the details of your new contacts?

How many times are you going to reach out and try to connect with them?

How will you do this follow-up so that you stand apart of other VAs and make a good first impression?

What are common questions you receive when you meet new prospects?

What details do you want to make sure you include in your response to these questions?

How will you respond to the question, "What do you do?"

What can you do to research your prospects before connecting with them (either in person or via email)?

CHAPTER FIVE

The Law of Attracting Clients?

Building relationships is the foundation to starting, maintaining and growing a successful business. If you're not building relationships, you'll find it difficult to find and retain clients.

It's important to remember that not all relationships will result in paying customers, but they will help you build your reputation, build your resources and become great referral sources at a later date.

THE KNOW, LIKE AND TRUST FACTOR

You have most likely heard the phrase "know, like and trust factor."
In order for people to do business with you, they first need to *know about you*. If they don't know about you, then they'll never contact you. This means you have to meet people – whether online or offline. (See Chapter 3 on building a presence for more on this.)

In order to continue building relationships, you need to keep in touch with your new contacts. I once received a great piece of advice from one of my clients, Sylva Leduc. She said that each time she attended a networking function and received a business card, she would quickly make a note on the back of the business card relating to the topics she had discussed with that person. The next day, she would either phone or email them and refer to this information. For example, if you've met someone who was interested in how long the VA industry has existed, you could follow up with them via email the next day with an article about the VA industry and its history. This allows you to reconnect with the person, remind them of who you are (remember, they probably met numerous people as well) and it also builds a relationship with your new contact.

As people get to know you, they're hopefully going to like you. If they like you – congratulate yourself – you're strengthening a new relationship. If they speak with others who need help with the services you provide, they may pass on your name and contact information.

Over time, as you continue building relationships, your contacts will trust you. Perhaps you will see this person at a monthly function, or you will exchange emails every few weeks or even meet for coffee in person. Of course you will only experience these benefits if you stay in touch.

"I DON'T KNOW WHAT I DON'T KNOW."

As Virtual Assistants, we often fail to realize that potential clients (and even our current clients in some cases) do not have the slightest clue of how we can really help them. They know what they want to achieve in their business, but in many cases, they don't know how to get there or how to get your help to get them there.

I want to introduce to you a statement a business owner made to me and my business partner, Tina Forsyth, during one of our "How to Boost Business with a VA" teleclasses.

"I don't know what I don't know."

When I heard this statement for the first time I thought, "What on earth does she mean?" As I thought about it some more, I realized what she was trying to tell me.

This statement so clearly demonstrates that many business owners really do not fully understand how a Virtual Assistant can help them.

It also emphasizes how critical it is for Virtual Assistant to fully understand what their prospects are hoping to accomplish within their business so they can "tell them what they don't know."

From the prospect's perspective, they know something is not working and it is most likely creating stress for them. By suggesting how you can help make their challenges easier, painless and potentially less expensive (i.e. telling them what they don't know), you are going to establish trust over time.

In order for our potential (and current) clients to "Know what they don't know" – we need to TELL them.

How do you even begin to tell your potential clients what they don't know and prove you are *the* best solution?

APPLYING "MINDSET" AND GAINING THEIR CONFIDENCE

In this section I want to focus on how you may be perceived and how you are presenting yourself as a Virtual Assistant and how you can apply your 'mindset' to gain confidence and build positive relationships with potential and current clients. We're going to talk about two kinds of 'mindset':

1. Business Mindset
2. Marketing Mindset

Business Mindset

In the last few months I have talked with Virtual Assistants about the transition of 'employee mindset' to 'business owner mindset'. Many VAs have already let me know that this item was helping them refocus themselves and build their business.

Many Virtual Assistants come from an administrative background in an office setting. In many cases, tasks were delegated and they made sure they took care of the needs of their managers. They were 'subordinates' within a hierarchy of a company and were told just want they needed to know. They were not always asked to provide feedback or input into the wider operations of the company. Basically, they did what they were told to do and were shown the resources they had to work with.

That old 'employee mentality' will not help you succeed as a professional Virtual Assistant or as a business owner. It takes a shift in thinking: from employee to business owner and applying the "Business Mindset". This is a transition many VAs find very difficult to overcome.

As a professional VA, your clients want more from you. They don't want to delegate every detail to you – they want you to delegate your own responsibilities. They want your feedback. They want you to share your ideas and hold them accountable. They may even want you to become a type of 'sidekick' to them.

If you're not able to live up to these expectations your client/VA relationship may become stale very quickly.

When a prospect shows interest and requests a time to speak with you to determine if you might be a good match to work together, this time is as much for you as it is for them. It's as much an opportunity for you to determine if this client is right for you as it is for them to determine if you're the right VA for them.

Transitioning to the Business Mindset - moving from the 'employee mentality' to the 'business owner mentality' can be challenging for many VAs, but it is critical for numerous reasons.

You are now a professional business owner and you want to work only with other professionals who are ready to work with you and ready for the expertise you provide. If you think of the preliminary call or meeting as an interview where you merely answer questions asked of you, you will not fully demonstrate your business mindset, or your full potential. You won't make as lasting of an impression as you could have. Also, you may not attract the type of client you really want to build a long-term relationship with.

By demonstrating your business mindset, your confidence in yourself, your business and in your expertise, you will attract those professionals who also offer this same level of confidence and expertise and who will value you.

Marketing Mindset

Marketing Mindset is defined as the ability to look ahead and understand a task so you can apply the appropriate technology or initiative, ask the appropriate questions, tell your client how you can help and take care of the rest. This is probably the #1 quality business owners look for in a VA. They do not describe it as Marketing Mindset but they will say *"I want a VA who will understand my business, thinks ahead and applies their initiative to take care of things so I don't have to."*

Applying the Marketing Mindset is what has built my business. I can honestly say that if I did not offer Marketing Mindset in my business, I would not have achieved growth and success in my business. This is a quality that many Virtual Assistants have, but are not utilizing. There are many other Virtual Assistants who prefer to "do

their job" and not think ahead and take on additional responsibilities. Marketing Mindset can take time to develop and you must be
comfortable in making use of it, however I cannot stress enough the
importance of applying this ingredient in your business.

The Marketing Mindset is directly related to "taking inventory".
By taking inventory you learn the details needed in order to apply
your Marketing Mindset.

When you 'take inventory" and apply your Marketing Mindset,
you are listening and gathering as much information about your
clients' business goals so that you can turn around and tell them
exactly how you can support them in achieving those goals. This
may sound simple, yet a very small percentage of VAs are applying
this in their daily conversations with current clients as well as new
clients.

Demonstrate your marketing mindset by taking the steps we
cover in this next section. We will start by preparing the prospect
for the preliminary appointment by asking the questions we need
to know in order to tell exactly what they need to know .... It will no
longer be a mystery to them.

Do you have Business Mindset and Marketing Mindset?

Score each question below from a scale of 1-5. 1 being 'not at all' and 5 'all the time'.

Do you:

1.	Apply your initiative when assisting your clients with tasks?	1	2	3	4	5
2.	Consider all pieces required to successfully achieve your clients' goals?	1	2	3	4	5
3.	Take inventory on a regular basis – determine your clients' short and long term goals and priorities – on a regular basis?	1	2	3	4	5
4.	Ask the right kind of questions to get critical details you need.	1	2	3	4	5
5.	Find out the answers to routine type of questions on your own.	1	2	3	4	5
6.	Tell your client how you can help?	1	2	3	4	5
7.	Create tasks lists and assign priorities to ensure the completion of a priority or goal?	1	2	3	4	5
8.	Keep your client accountable and track deadlines?	1	2	3	4	5
9.	Keep up-to-date with current trends, technology and resources?	1	2	3	4	5
10.	Brainstorm and provide feedback to your client on a regular basis?	1	2	3	4	5
11.	Keep in regular communication with your client – via email and phone?	1	2	3	4	5
12.	Take care of routine tasks so your client doesn't have to even think about them?	1	2	3	4	5
13.	Provide your client with confidence in you in order to continue in developing the relationship	1	2	3	4	5
14.	Provide support in business building related tasks (and not just administrative type tasks)	1	2	3	4	5
15.	Provide a good return on your client's monthly investment of your services?	1	2	3	4	5

Score table:

If you scored 1-25

Applying your mindset is critical to finding and retaining clients. Invest time in yourself and implement the mindset strategy in to you your business ASAP.

If you scored 26-50

You are using a little bit of mindset but you could certainly use a lot more. Add a few more strategies into your business and you will notice a difference.

If you scored 50-75

Congratulations, you are applying mindset in your practice. Keep in mind any of the areas you are not currently using and you will see improvement. You are already offering so much more than many other virtual assistants.

C H A P T E R   S I X

Taking Inventory

PREP YOUR PROSPECT FOR THE PRELIMINARY APPOINTMENT

In order to effectively help your clients, you need to know what, specifically, their goals are for their business

You could start by having prospects complete a 'Client Application Form', just like the one we use in the Multiple Streams Team. (See Appendix for a copy of the Client Application form).

The preliminary interview is the perfect opportunity for you to learn about your client, the direction of their business and exactly how you can help them grow and demonstrate your business and marketing mindset.

Start by asking the prospect to get ready for the call. Before your call, send them an email confirming the time and date of the appointment and let them know what you would like to accomplish during the call. This sets the stage to ensure you get what you need from the interview.

Below is a sample email I send to potential clients to confirm their appointment as well as identify what I want to cover during the call:

Hi [client name],
I am looking forward to speaking with you about how I may be able to assist you with your growing business.

*Just to confirm, our time is scheduled for [**date and time (always include time zone)**]*

During our call (15-20 minutes) I'd like to learn about:
- *You and your business,*
- *Your business goals,*
- *Your priority projects and*
- *Your expectations of a VA.*

Before our call, please take a few minutes to think about these items so we can make the most of our time together.

Of course I'd also be happy to answer your questions about working with a VA and about myself and my business.

I look forward to connecting with you.

Regards,

[your signature block]

There are four specific benefits to 'setting the stage' by sending this email to your prospect in preparation for your preliminary interview.

1. You **show your professionalism and initiative** in preparing for the call.
2. You **provide them with content to consider ahead of time** – this makes better use of your time together.
3. You **demonstrate your expertise and professionalism**.
4. You **tell them you know how you can best help them** – by gathering the specifics of their particular situation you have an opportunity to demonstrate how you can apply your solutions accordingly.

In order for you to completely understand if you have the skills, knowledge and expertise to assist this person and build a successful long-term relationship (and to confirm you want to work with them), you need to know and understand what they want to accomplish with their business as well as what challenges they are experiencing.

Once you know this, you can make an informed decision as to whether this is a client you want to work with and if you have the right skills to assist them with building their business.

Remember – when a prospect shows interest and requests a time to speak with you. It's as much an opportunity for you to determine if this client is right for you as it is for them to determine if you're the right VA for them.

Just because someone has expressed interest in learning more about you and potentially working with you does not mean the decision is only in their hands. If you are a new VA, you may think you should (and need) to accept every potential client that expresses interest in working with you. This is not the case.

WHAT IS TAKING INVENTORY?

'Taking Inventory' simply means learning all the critical details about your potential client in order to <u>tell</u> them how you can help them. The best time to take inventory is during the initial call with your potential client.

Note the emphasis above on the word 'tell'. You're not going to ask your clients, "How can I help you?" Once you know enough about what they want for their business, you're going to <u>tell</u> them how you can help them. Basically, you are going to 'tell them what they don't know'.

So how do you do that?

In order to provide the best support possible to your clients, you need to know several things:

- What services and products do they offer?
- Who is their target market?
- What are their goals? (short term and long term)
- What are their priorities?
- What expectations do they have of a VA?

By gathering these details, you put yourself in a position where you can easily tell the client what you can do to help them achieve their goals.

If you don't take inventory, you will not have the same amount of detail to directly relate how the solutions you will provide will minimize the potential client's challenges.

This step is absolutely critical and can be the difference between getting new clients or not.

My Story...

In the last few years, I've worked closely with members, both clients and VAs of the Multiple Streams Team.

One particular scenario stands apart as a great example of the difference between a VA who asks their clients how they can help and a VA who tells their clients how they can help.

Mary, a VA on the Multiple Streams Team, was matched up with Anne, a Multiple Streams Team client. For months, their relationship went nowhere. It was a struggle for Mary to receive work from Anne and Anne felt frustrated that she wasn't receiving the rewards she thought she should be experiencing by having a VA work with her.

They were both frustrated and I needed to understand why, to help move this situation forward.

I spoke with both Anne and Mary separately and they voiced their concerns about each other. When I spoke with Mary, I asked her to tell me exactly what she would say to her client Anne, when she spoke with her each week. She told me they reviewed her priorities and assigned deadlines to a few tasks. At the end of every discussion, Mary would always ask, "Anne, how else can I help you?"

Anne, a client who 'didn't know what she didn't know' would say, "Let me think about it -- I'll get back to you."

When I heard Mary's question, "How else can I help you?", I immediately realized what was going on. Mary was *asking* Anne how she could help her rather than taking inventory and *telling* Anne exactly how she could best help her. Mary wasn't a solution to Anne's challenges. She wasn't telling Anne 'what she didn't know'. She was expecting tasks to be delegated to her from her client - someone who really had no idea how her VA could help her best. She was not employing her Business Mindset or her Marketing Mindset.

This is a common scenario experienced by business owners and Virtual Assistants alike, and it can be frustrating for all concerned.

Once we uncovered what was taking place, I coached Mary on how to 'take inventory' from her client and let her know specifically how she could help. Over time their relationship grew and they now look back and laugh at how they started out.

Let's take a more thorough look at why taking inventory during the preliminary interview is so critical:

ABOUT THEIR BUSINESS

It's important to know about your client's business so you can fully understand where they are coming from. You can often get these details from their website, but it's helpful to have your potential client tell you, in their own words, what their business is really all about. Be sure they include details about:

- Who they work with.
- What services they offer.
- What products they offer.

As you listen to your potential client, make notes and start thinking about whether this is your ideal client.

Ask yourself:

- Are you interested in this type of business?
- Are you the right person for this role?
- Do you feel excitement about what they do?
- Can you see yourself working in this kind of business long-term?
- Do you feel a personal connection to this person?

ABOUT THEIR TARGET MARKET

It's important to get a really good understanding of your potential clients' target market. If their target market is very broad say, for example, women professionals, it may be very difficult for you to later assist with researching places online to reach this market. Try to get the target market as specific as possible.

Early in the book, I mentioned how defining a target market can be a challenging task for any business owner. Explain to your client why it's so important for you to know who their specific market is in order for you to best assist them.

Ask yourself:

- Are you interested in and comfortable with working with this market?
- Do you know enough about them to fully support your client?
- How can you become more familiar with this target market?

WHAT ARE THEIR GOALS?

Clients want their VAs to be able to look ahead and help them achieve their goals. In order to do this, it's critical to be aware of both their short and long term goals. By knowing your client's specific goals, you can start to think ahead, visualize and therefore *tell* your client how you can help them accomplish the goals. There is nothing more powerful than being able to confidently tell your potential client how you can help them achieve a goal that may have seemed so distant to them – before they met you of course.

If your potential client provides you with very general goals, such as, "I want to make more money" ask them how they want to make more money: By creating more products? By adding more group coaching programs? Knowing *how* they want to make more money helps you identify how you can help them generate more money.

Ask yourself:

- How can I contribute to the success and accomplishment of these goals?
- Do I feel I understand why these goals are important to them and how they fit into the growth of the business?
- Are the goals specific enough that I can identify various tasks that are required in order to achieve the goal?
- What programs, systems and technology are required in order to reach these goals?
- What kind of research, resources (or other details) are required to achieve these goals?
- How can these goals be broken down in to smaller tasks?

My Story...

One day I asked a potential client, "What are your goals between now and the end of the year ... what do you want to accomplish?" Their response was, "make more money." Not a surprise: everyone wants to make more money. This was not the answer I needed. With this response, I could not tell them specifically how I could help them make more money if I didn't know *how* they wanted to do it.

I said, "Okay, so how will you make more money? What will you create in order to do this?

Then they started talking about how they wanted to create a membership site. They wanted to develop a group coaching program, an ebook, etc. Bingo! This is exactly what I was looking for – the specifics of *what* so I could tell them *how* I could help.

Now that I knew what they wanted to create in their product funnel, I could think ahead and make a note about how I could play a role in accomplishing those goals.

When they were done, telling me their goals (of course I documented them), I said, "Awesome! You know, I helped someone recently with setting up a group coaching program – I can look after numerous things…" and I listed off half a dozen items I could take on that would help in accomplishing this goal.

See what I did here? I shared my experience and also how I could think ahead. I told her how I could help rather than *asking* her how I could help her. I applied both my Business Mindset and Marketing Mindset.

WHAT ARE THEIR PRIORITIES?

Learning about your clients' immediate priorities is especially important when starting a new relationship because it gives you a place to start. If you know only the long-term goals, how will you know what is important to them now? If you don't know what's important now, how can you help them reach their long-term goals?

Business owners are busy. Remember, because they 'don't know what they don't know', they don't realize the investment they are making when starting to work with a new VA.

By asking your client what their priorities are for the next week, next two weeks or for the next month, you can break down those priorities into smaller tasks. After that you can ask questions to gather the details you need to know and then *tell* your client what you can and can't (or won't) take on.

If your potential client is new to working with a VA and does not yet fully understand how to get started working with you, you may want to suggest getting started with a priority project they haven't had time to do. For example, perhaps they need help setting up a shopping cart or researching details for their next ezine or product. By having a smaller project to get started with, it allows for the development of the relationship and enhances the trust of both the client and the VA. If the client finds it challenging to 'give up' certain tasks, working on smaller projects will strengthen their trust and over time be more comfortable with 'letting go.'

My Story...

A few years ago I was referred to a business coach who needed VA support. At the time he didn't know me well although he highly trusted a client of mine who had referred me. We decided to get started slowly.

He asked me to help with an article submission project. He gave me a few articles and had me find places online to submit them and track where they were posted. We met by phone every few weeks and I kept a tracking sheet of every place I had submitted his articles and where they were posted.

Over time, I had exhausted many of the free article submission sites so I got creative and started researching other websites I could potentially submit his articles to – places that did not normally take articles, but where the article content was in direct alignment with the website copy and topic. I emailed the website owner, introduced myself, told them why I was contacting them and asked if they were interested in my client's article. I was successful many times and managed to get my client's article posted to many additional places other than the usual article directories.

Without even realizing it, I had applied the Business Mindset and Marketing Mindset. I knew my client wanted his name to appear on as many websites as possible and so I looked 'outside the box' to do my best at supporting the success of this goal.

My client not only appreciated my efforts, he appreciated the fact that I had applied my initiative and mindset to help him achieve his goal. I had gained his trust and he was ready to have me work on more with him.

Soon after I started to work on more projects, take on more responsibility and became an essential part of his team.

WHAT ARE THEIR EXPECTATIONS?

Expectations. It can be a loaded word, often with negative overtones to it. Perhaps that's why discussing expectations is avoided by so many VAs and potential clients when first discussing the possibility of working together.

Expectations can mean anything from:

- Hours of work.
- Response time to email correspondence and phone messages.
- Turn around time on projects.
- Confidentiality.
- Rates.
- How they would like your help in keeping them accountable.

Imagine you start a new relationship with a client and you have not discussed expectations. The client emails you with a request and does not include a deadline in the email. You assume it's not an urgent request and you add the task to your 'to-do' list.

The next morning you receive another email from the same client indicating not to worry about the task they had sent you – they did it themselves. You get that feeling in the pit of your stomach as if something may not be quite right. Perhaps you're even annoyed that your client went ahead and just took care of the tasks themselves.

When you speak next, the client tells you they were disappointed that you had not completed the task as quickly as they would have liked. You're surprised – the email didn't indicate urgency and it hadn't even been 24 hours since you received the email.

Had you spoken about turn around time and deadline expectations, this situation may have been avoided.

It's critical to have upfront and ongoing discussions about expectations – both your and your clients'.

My business partner, Tina Forsyth, and I wrote an article entitled, "How to Communicate with Your VA (or your client)" - (you can find this article in the Appendix section and also at at **www.MultipleStreamsTeam.com/articles.html)**

In it, we outline very specific items a VA and potential client (or current client) should discuss at the beginning of their relationship. Issues such as, hours of work, preferred method of communication, turn around time on deadlines, requests etc.

If you're not communicating clearly with your potential and current clients about expectations, I strongly encourage you to do so. If not, you may experience a frustrating and difficult situation that could have been avoided had you spoken and clarified it from the beginning.

Once a relationship is 'damaged', due to a misunderstanding between you and your client, it can be difficult to repair. As the VA, it's up to you to connect with your client and let them know you'd like to confirm you both have the same understanding of expectations between the two of you.

Another item to discuss may be around your clients' expectations of your relationship as a whole. I recently had a discussion with a business owner who indicated she wanted to experience return on investment from her VA within the very first month of working with her.

Business owners evaluate return-on-investment differently. Some may evaluate it based on generated revenue and others may identify how the VA support may not have generated monetary gains immediately, but over time, will certainly contribute to the growth of the business.

Depending on your potential clients' expectations of you and how they assess return-on-investment, you may need to clarify realistic expectations.

I often describe the first one to three months of a new client/VA relationship as the 'dating stage'. Both parties are becoming familiar with one another, sharing details about each other, investing time to fully understand the business, goals, target market and overall style of the business as well as implementing systems. During this time, there is certainly time to take care of various tasks, however the client may not experience immediate monetary results and therefore question the relationship.

By discussing this as part of your preliminary conversation, you can understand and clarify or (if needed) educate your client on realistic expectations.

Make sure your potential client has accurate expectations of your role. Your role as a Virtual Assistant should not be confused with the role of a Marketing Director, Coach or anything other than what a VA does. Read my article "What a VA Is and Is Not" for more information on this.

ARE YOU THE RIGHT VA?

Once you gather these details about the potential client, you can sit back and consider whether this client is right for you or not. Remember, the preliminary interview is also for you to determine if this client is right for you – there is no obligation to move forward if you don't feel it's the right decision.

If you feel hesitation or that 'feeling in the pit of your stomach' – listen to that feeling. Not every client is the 'ideal client' for you. We all have our own individual personalities and if you're not the right match for someone, there's no reason to force it. If you do force a relationship, you will regret it later – I guarantee it.

Ask yourself these questions:

- Are you excited about the possibility of working with them?
- Does the work they do excite you?
- Are you comfortable with the target market?
- Is this person an 'ideal client' for you?
- Do you feel a personal connection with this client?
- Can you see yourself working with this client on a long-term basis?
- Do you see potential growth and development of your role in the business?
- Do you feel the client will welcome your feedback?
- Do you feel the client respects your boundaries?
- Are you comfortable with the expectations of your client?
- Is the client ready to work with a VA?
- Is the client clear on how they want to build their business?
- Does the client fully understand the role of a VA (versus expecting a Marketing Director, Coach etc.)?
- Can he/she afford you?
- Do you offer the skills required to work with this client?

IS THIS POTENTIAL CLIENT AN 'IDEAL' CLIENT?

It can take time, but after speaking with a few potential clients, you may become very familiar with key factors that will help you determine if this prospect may be an ideal client for you.

In my role with the Multiple Streams Team, I can usually tell, within the first 15 minutes of speaking with a prospect, whether they are an ideal client for our team or not.

Ideal Client	May Not Yet be an Ideal Client
• Is able to clearly communicate their business goals.	• Is unclear with business goals or communicates general goals, such as 'make more money' or 'get more clients'.
• Has appropriate expectations of the Virtual Assistant.	• Wants the Virtual Assistant to guide, lead and manage the growth of the business.
• Understands and values the VA skill, expertise and, therefore rates.	• Is 'stuck' on the VA rate and isn't comfortable spending the money for the help.
• Understands and values the time it takes to complete tasks appropriately.	• Continuously questions the amount of time required to complete tasks.
• Is looking for a long term relationship and eventual 'partnership' from their VA.	• Needs help with projects here and there and wants to be trained on how to complete various tasks.
• Is comfortable and trusts VA with taking over and managing tasks as appropriate.	• Feels they need to micromanage and check over every detail completed.
• Openly shares details about the business, goals, priorities, resources, etc.	• Provides direction on specific items only and is tight on providing additional business details.
• Creates time in calendar to communicate verbally with the VA.	• Is too busy to make time to connect verbally with the VA.

If you feel uncertain or uncomfortable with your discussion or specific details about your potential client, make note of these and be true to yourself in whether you feel you will have a successful and fulfilling relationship with them. Listen to your instinct – it's most likely accurate – and it will save you frustration and stress later on.

If you don't feel you are the right VA to work with a prospect – do not feel badly. Not every business owner is meant to work with every VA. We all have different personalities, traits, expectations and tolerations. Let them know you don't feel you are the right VA for them and refer them to a colleague who you feel may be the right person, or VA organization where they can meet other potential VAs.

Many times Virtual Assistants may feel the genuine need to assist someone with their challenges. However, as professional business owners, we also need to consider ourselves first.

Exercise:

Is this client "Ideal" for you?

- They are within your target market.
- You feel a connection with their personality, their target market and the direction of their business.
- You feel your skills will contribute to the growth of their business.
- You can speak and understand their language.
- You have a full understanding of their goals and priorities.
- You don't experience the "gut feeling" telling you this isn't a good match.
- You feel they respect you and value what you bring to their business.
- You are excited about the goals they have identified for their business.

Next time you speak with a client (new or current) you can try using the following script template to demonstrate your mindset:

For New Clients:

"Tell me **about your business**. I'd like to learn more about you, your background and your niche."

"Can you share with me what you want to accomplish with your business? What are you **goals** for the next six months?"

"If we were to start working together, what would be the first three to five **priorities** you would have me assist you with?"

"What are your **expectations**?"

"Define for me what the perfect VA looks like to you."

"Are you looking for a short or long term support?"

"How many hours do you think you may require each week/each month?"

Exercise:

For Current Clients (assuming you already know about their business and niche)**:**

"Let's talk about your business goals. What are you **goals** for the next six months?"

"What your priorities for the next week/next 2 weeks/next month?"

"What are your **expectations of me**? Let me share with you what I need from you in order to do my job well."

"What is currently working really well with our relationship?"

"What would you like to see done differently in our relationship?"

CHAPTER SEVEN

Sign on the Dotted Line

When a potential client says, "I am very interested in working with you. How do we get started?" and you feel that you, too, would like to work with them…

What do you do next?

Well, first you might get off your computer (or phone) and jump around with excitement and celebrate. Then what?

In order to maintain your level of professionalism, you will want to ensure you have a few things in place to easily and quickly start working with a new client. These include a:

- Client Agreement.
- Invoice Template.
- Time Tracking Software (easily keeps track of your time and projects).
- Weekly summary of tasks and hours template.
- Seamless method for your clients to process payments.
- Communication Plan with items to discuss.

Before you officially begin a relationship with any clients, I strongly encourage you to have an agreement in place, signed by both you and the client. This agreement should include items such as confidentiality, rates, summary of items you will be assisting with etc.

There are various agreements available on the Internet that you can customize for your own business. I have included a sample in the Appendix for you to review.

By having an agreement in place, it confirms you and your client have the same understanding of one another. If an issue is raised, you can go back to the agreement to confirm what was agreed upon from the start.

My Story...

I had an agreement with all of my clients, so why I decided I didn't need it with one client in particular, I'm not sure. This experience proved to be one of the most important lessons I learned.

I met a local business coach at a networking event and we immediately clicked. She had a great personality and in the back of my mind I knew I would work with her some day.

The very next day this same coach sent me an urgent "help" email asking that I contact her immediately – she desperately needed assistance.

I called her right away and started working immediately on her project. She had a tight deadline – there wasn't time to talk about rates, confidentiality, communication or much else.

A couple of weeks later our relationship completely broke down. I had sent her an invoice for my services and shortly after I received a horrific email from this client stating how dare I charge this rate and if I planned to have a successful business, I would think twice about charging this amount (the hourly rate was $25/hour).

My calls and emails to this client were left unanswered for days.

I was bewildered, upset and irate. I immediately started to doubt myself, my services and my worth.

Finally my client connected with me, indicated my rate was much too high and she could not work with me at this rate.

I remember how my confidence dropped significantly and I regrettably lowered my rate and continued to work with this client. I then advised I needed a signed agreement in place (confirming the lower hourly rate) in order for us to continue working together.

As you might imagine, the problems with this client didn't stop here. I wish I could say we ended the relationship amicably, but we did not. However, I am grateful for learning a valuable lesson.

Looking back, I'm not sure why I continued working with this client or why I felt I needed to revise my invoice to accommodate her. Like many VAs, I genuinely cared and wanted to help this client – even at my own expense.

Even though this situation was difficult, it made me realize the critical importance of having:

- a client agreement in place.
- clear communication at the beginning of a new client relationship

It also made me realize I was a professional business owner who offered professional services of tremendous value and I would only work with those who also recognized this value.

ENSURING A SUCCESSFUL RELATIONSHIP

Send the agreement to your client, ask them to review it, sign it and return it so you can sign it also. Do not start any work until you receive the agreement back. This formalizes your relationship, demonstrates you are a professional and serious about your business and it also ensures you both have the same understanding of your working relationship.

Once the agreement is signed and returned, I would request a payment to get started. You may ask your clients to purchase an, 'introductory plan' of some kind – perhaps purchasing 10 hours that can be used over 60 days. This confirms your client's commitment to working with you and also to get them used to paying for hours ahead of time, rather than after the fact. If you plan to retain your clients and have them move on to a monthly retainer plan, this will be helpful to put in place from the start.

Once the agreement is signed and you have received your first payment, you're ready to get started. Schedule a time to connect with your client by phone and move forward, referring back to the inventory details you took on your preliminary call.

Note: Remember your client may not 'know what they don't know' so they may find it difficult to know how to get started working with you. Your client will appreciate (and most likely need) you to take the lead on how to get your new relationship started.

On the first official call with your client, there are usually a lot of issues to talk over. Make sure you are prepared. During this call, I suggest you ask questions: let your client do most of the talking and listen to what it is they need. Once you do this, you are in a much better position to tell them exactly how you can assist them with each of the priorities and also create a list of tasks that need to be completed to finalize the priority project.

A priority for your client may be something as simple as wanting to get a regular newsletter out to their database.

Perhaps they are challenged with making the time to write the articles. Think about any other items they may want to include in the newsletter then format it and send it out.

As a VA – this is an easy task for you to help with. Here are some things you may consider:

- Ask your client when he/she would like the newsletters to go out each month and create a schedule.
- Confirm the method your client uses to distribute the newsletter.
- In the schedule, include the date that your client needs to get the newsletter copy to you by (usually 4-5 days before the distribution date).
- Schedule reminders for yourself so you keep on track with sending the newsletter, but also for keeping your client accountable (to make sure you receive the content from them on time).
- Ask if you can assist with any research, gathering details, perhaps drafting some areas if you are comfortable.
- When you receive the newsletter copy from your client:
  - Proofread.
  - Enter it into the newsletter template.
  - Create tracking links as appropriate.
  - Send a draft to yourself, fully review and test the links.
  - Send a draft for your client to review.
- Once approved, send the newsletter to your client's database.

There are likely a few additional steps I would add in the list above, but this provides you with a quick example of how easily you, the professional VA, can directly and easily impact the growth of your client's business, even by supporting a simple task like distributing an ezine.

By applying your marketing mindset, using your initiative and your skills, you are proving to your client that you are an important factor in the success of her business. This is the benefit that, over time, will provide you with a retainer client who will continue to work with you on an ongoing basis.

IMPLEMENTING THE MINDSET

1. Write out a summary of your client's immediate priorities. During your initial discussion, be sure to talk to your client about their top priorities. These priorities may be the same ones they shared with you during their preliminary interview, or they may have changed. Listen to the details your client shares with you about each one. Think about how you can apply your newfound mindset to assist your client with each item.

2. Create the Task List. Your client has shared their immediate priorities and now it's time for you to discuss the tasks that need to be completed in order to finalize the priority project. Share with them the tasks you can take over and also add tasks they need to complete. Ask them how they prefer to be kept accountable to ensure they look after the items they need to complete. Document these items and send a summary to your client after the call with the details (many clients will greatly appreciate this). Make note of the deadlines in your own calendar so they aren't forgotten.

3. Your Communication Plan. This is a critical step, yet one that many VAs and clients do not take the time to do. Everyone has personal preferences when it comes to methods of communication. When looking to create a long-term relationship with your new client, it's very important that you discuss how you will communicate with each other. Some people prefer regular communication by phone, some by email. Some clients want to pick up the phone at any time throughout the day and call their VA. Some VAs require

very flexible schedules and don't work a standard 9-5 work week.
I strongly recommend (at least in the beginning of your relationship) that you connect by phone once a week. This gives you voice-to-voice connection and the opportunity to speak directly about priorities, goals, accomplishments, issues, etc.

Email is usually the preferred form of daily communication. Many VAs and clients also use instant messaging throughout the day.

You may find yourself communicating differently with each client. As long as it works for both of you – that's all that matters.

In the Appendix I have included an article called, "Communicating with your VA (or Client)." which outlines several communication areas to consider in your new relationship. I strongly encourage you to discuss this with your client at the beginning of your relationship to avoid any frustration later on.

Here are examples of what I have seen:

Client has expected to receive a response that an email was received and confirmation of when task will be completed.	VA has read the email, added the item to their to-do list and not acknowledged to their client that they received the email and when it will be completed.
Client has sent an email with a task and expected it to be completed immediately (but did not include a deadline).	VA has read the email, added it to their to-do list, not realizing the client needed the task to be completed immediately.
Client continuously calls outside of scheduled appointments with the VA.	VA schedule requires flexibility due to other obligations (children, part-time employment etc.) and is available primarily for scheduled calls only.
Client would like to see weekly record of tasks completed and time used to help in identifying better revenue generating ways to have the VA support.	VA does not provide regular updates of time used or projects completed.

Dealing with communication issues is very stressful and can damage a client/VA relationship. Communicate about communication -- Make a point of discussing communication to prevent problems now, and in the future in your business relationships.

My Story...

This is a real-life example of a situation I was involved with, via a VA and client. The VA and client were partnered together – they really enjoyed their partnership. The VA's skills were well matched to the tasks the client needed help with.

The client was really busy and unable to commit to regular phone calls with the VA. The VA had 2 small children and completed most of her work in the evening hours. She also had numerous clients she was also supporting.

They corresponded mostly via email.

The client started to feel frustrated with the time it took for the VA to respond to her emails. She was hoping to receive acknowledgement of the email within just a few hours of it being sent (they had not communicated this).

The VA felt overwhelmed by all the emails her client sent her on a daily basis with items that needed urgent attention. More and more, the VA was finding it difficult to balance her other work, her children and responding to her client's emails as quickly as she would like.

The relationship slowly started to deteriorate.

The client eventually called me to say she needed a new VA because, although she really liked her, she didn't feel they were the right fit.

I asked her the following questions:

- How have you and how are you communicating (email, regular phone conversation, other)?
- What are your expectations of your VA with regards to email response time, project completion and is this information included in your emails to her?
- Did you and the VA discuss your expectations of one another – including response turn-around, communication and, hours of work for example?

The client told me they were communicating strictly by email, she expected a response from the VA within the same business day, and no, they had not talked specifically about communication when they started working together.

I immediately knew why they were both experiencing this frustration.

They had not discussed any of the "communication plan" items that are critical in starting a new relationship. Even though they were corresponding via email, they really were not communicating at all. They had not invested time in one another and had little understanding of what the other person was experiencing.

I scheduled a time to speak with both the client and the VA and we discussed what had taken place as well as what they each expected from one another. Within a short time, both sides compromised and agreed to specific methods of communication and moved forward in their relationship. Once they had this open discussion and understood one another a little more, their relationship grew and they are still working together today.

Don't fall victim to frustration due to not taking time to chat about your communication plan -- make it a priority in your first call.

Exercise:

Communicating With Your Client
Items to discuss with all clients when you start
working together.

1. What are your working hours?

2. What are your clients working hours?

3. When is the best time to reach you?

4. When is the best time to reach your client?

5. How do you prefer to communicate? (email, telephone, instant messenger)

6. How does your client prefer to communicate? (email, telephone, instant messenger)

7. I recommend connecting with your client, at the very least, once a month. (I personally like to connect even for 20 minutes once a week by phone with clients). Then use email to manage most communication around projects/tasks. What communication combination will you suggest to your client?

8. How often would you like to meet with your client(s)?

9. How often would your client like to meet with you?

10. How will you be providing regular updates to your client on hours used, tasks completed etc.

11. On your scheduled calls, determine:

- Top priorities for the next week/2 weeks and their deadlines.
- Top 3 projects for the month and their deadlines.
- The goals for the month and following month.
- Create a master "project" list and quickly update it.
- Who is responsible for tasks related to each deadline?

CHAPTER EIGHT

Keep Them Coming Back for More

One of the most common questions VAs ask me is, "How do I build long-term relationships with my clients and keep them coming back month after month?"

I had made the assumption that most VAs have long-term client relationships, so I was shocked to read in the VA Networking Survey that more than 78% of Virtual Assistants turn over less than 10% of their clients each month. Visit http://www.vanetworking.com/survey/ for additional details.

What this means is that the majority of Virtual Assistants are continuously in need of finding new clients each month. Why? Because they aren't building long-term, consistent relationships with clients who have committed to a monthly retainer.

If you are:

- taking inventory regularly;
- applying your marketing mindset;
- keeping good communication, and;
- working on tasks that contribute to the growth of your client's business

I can almost guarantee you that you will create long-term, retainer relationships with these clients.

Business owners want a 'sidekick' to work with on building their business. They want to experience value and they want to feel like they are the only person you are working with. Give them value, make them feel they are your top priority and help them build their business and generate revenue and they WILL work with you for many years to come.

ARE YOU INVALUABLE?

In the teleclass, my business partner Tina and I offer "Boost Business with a Virtual Assistant", we share specific ways business owners can use VAs to help them 'boost business'. For example, instead of having a VA focus on administrative tasks such as booking appointments etc., identify ways the VA can contribute to business building activities within the business, such as list building types of activities. List-building is defined as strategies you and your client use to bring traffic to your website to convert as members to your client's database. For example, article marketing, submitting press releases, joint ventures etc.

Through the Multiple Streams Team, I also offer complimentary brainstorm sessions to our own MST clients and their VA to identify additional ways the VA can help the client in their business. We want the clients to see their VA as an **invaluable investment in their business rather than an expense**.

Both the teleclasses and brainstorm sessions have been very successful in assisting not only business owners and clients, but also helping VAs think "outside the box" on how they can apply their mindset towards their clients business.

Ask yourself these questions:

- Do you apply your Marketing Mindset in the work you do with your clients?
- Do you fully understand your clients' short and long-term business goals?
- Do you understand the strategies and business model they are following to accomplish their goals?
- Do you ask your clients the right questions, and tell them how you will help them achieve their goals?
- Do you provide feedback and suggestions as appropriate?
- Do you challenge them when they speak with you about changing priorities and direction of their business?
- Are you continuing to build your skill, your experience and expertise in areas that make a difference to them?

As you and your client move forward in your relationship, you will become more familiar with everything to do with their business.

If you answered yes to the questions above, you will have <u>no problem</u> with retaining your clients.

If you answered 'no' to the questions above, take the time to listen to what your client needs you to contribute. Complete research, ask questions: show them you are interested in learning about various pieces so you can increase the support you offer to them. By reading this book and applying the various steps outlined, you should be able to put these into place with no problem.

As you continue applying your marketing mindset, you will continue to:

- Build a stronger relationship with your clients.
- Increase your hours with specific clients.
- Hire additional VA contractors to assist you with client work or,

- Stop working with clients that cannot offer the same kind of commitment.
- Negotiate higher fees.

SEAMLESS PAYMENT PROCESSING

When we pay for something of value and the process is automated, we don't usually give the amount of money it costs much thought – we know how much it cost, we see the value of it and we are willing to pay for it. However, when we pay for something of value and the process is *not* automated – meaning, we need to take some sort of action to pay for the item, there is a window of opportunity to think twice about our purchase. We may second-guess whether the item is of value or not.

The same goes for ongoing processing of payments for your clients.

If you have your clients on a monthly retainer plan, I encourage you to have a completely seamless (and somewhat invisible) method to collect payments each month.

By setting up a recurring payment option in a shopping cart system, the transaction will take place each month automatically on a specific date and be deposited into your account. If you invoice your client and they need to manually submit payment each month, you may not receive payment as quickly and it may prompt somewhat of a negotiation discussion each month.

Having a seamless method to process your client payments is not meant as a way to hide billing details from your client, rather it's a way to implement automation and technology.

My Story...

A few years ago I sent a client a PayPal invoice for the next month's retainer plan. Several days had gone by and the invoice had not been paid. This was normal – not intentional, but normal. I contacted my client and asked if they had any questions about the invoice. They responded by letting me they didn't have any questions, but it was just one more thing they had to do amongst their numerous other priorities. Even though it was literally a 2 second task, they still found it difficult to get it taken care of. They suggested that as a business owner with a growing business that I should consider implementing some form of recurring payment system so I would receive my payment on time and they wouldn't have to think about paying the invoice or the funds they were spending.

I eventually introduced a shopping cart system to my business and completely automated the payment process for all of my clients. They appreciated this and I certainly appreciated receiving my payments on time!

BUILDING LONG-TERM

Building your business and your expertise to a point where you are receiving all kinds of interest for your services is very powerful. You may feel more comfortable in turning away business that is outside of what you really enjoy. You may also find you are taking on more and more responsibilities with your clients and increasing your hours significantly with certain clients.

How do you continue providing even more support with the same number of hours in a day?

You don't. In fact, you can't.

This is a point I have experienced and I have seen many Virtual Assistants reach. They have several clients, all requiring more from them, and they don't know what to do. They don't want to let anyone down and they certainly don't want to give away any of the revenue they are generating.

Unless you participate in a scientific experiment of some kind – you cannot clone yourself (believe me, I've tried!) so it's time to make changes.

This can be a very difficult stage. You may not be in a position to hire your own VA support yet, you can't keep up with time required to effectively look after your clients.

You need to make a decision. Either you:

- Hire a VA to subcontract to.
- Hire an employee.
- Downsize your client base.
- Start losing track of your work and losing clients because they can feel you are 'too busy'.

The last item is really not an option. No matter what, you need to maintain the same, if not an increased level of support to your clients.

Hiring a VA to subcontract to and/or downsizing your client base are most likely the options that make the most sense.

My Story...

When I reached the position in my business where I had just too much work, I panicked a little. How was I going to support my clients, continue to take on more responsibilities and have a life outside of my business – all at the same time? It was one of the hardest points of my VA business. I wanted to make sure I maintained at least the same amount of income every month – I couldn't give that up. I also had a great personal relationship with all my clients – I really liked them and was disappointed to think I may upset them by not continuing to work with them.

My business partner Tina Forsyth was invaluable to me at this time. She helped me through the process of deciding how I was going to downsize my clients, yet generate the same revenue (if not more) each month.

I started by making a list of all of my clients. I noted the current hours I was supporting them and the payment they made to me each month.

I then connected with a VA who had worked with me on various projects and asked her if she would be open to taking on some of my clients as I was 'downsizing'. She agreed. We set up a compensation plan so I would receive a small referral fee from her.

For clients that could not commit to a retainer plan of at least 10 hours a month, I decided I was going to let them know I was making changes in my business and had another VA who I knew would take good care of them. This was very emotionally challenging to prepare for because I genuinely cared for these people and didn't want to create any additional stress for them.

I contacted each client by phone to let them know about my decision. I made a point of sharing with them that this was a business decision I needed to make and I wanted to ensure they would be looked after. I told them I had already made arrangements with another VA, should they feel comfortable with connecting and moving forward with her.

These clients were very supportive and understanding (phew!) of my decision. This, of course, made it much easier for me.

I also shared this 'downsizing' news with the clients I was going to keep. I wanted them to feel confident I was going to continue working with them and also let them know that I would be available for additional hours if needed. I also let them know that as I had increased my expertise in various areas and was no longer able (or willing) to take on additional clients I wanted to discuss new potential compensation plans with them. This was another difficult topic for me to bring up, but it needed to be done.

These changes made a significant positive difference in my relationship with my clients.

When you reach the point where you need to downsize in your own business, listen to yourself. If you don't, the consequences could be burn out, illness and/or a loss of business in the end.

You may need support during this transition in your business. Find someone who you can speak to about the decisions you need to make. It's best not to discuss this with your spouse or close family member. Choose someone who understands your business and what you may be experiencing.

Take your time in making your decisions and in your downsizing and sub-contracting process. You do not need to do everything at once, but you should be clear on what you want to accomplish in the end.

RETAINING YOUR CLIENTS

If you can prove that you are invaluable, your client will keep you around for a long time. Check off the statements below that you are currently offering to your clients.

Clients want a VA who is:

- ☑ Going to **think ahead of them** and take care of the details (by applying the 'mindset').
- ☑ **Familiar** with their business and their business goals.
- ☑ Able to **strategically apply common online systems** to automate and build their business.
- ☑ Able to **apply their expertise** and assist in generating revenue.
- ☑ **Confident** in their work.
- ☑ **Comfortable providing suggestions** and feedback.
- ☑ Going to tell them how they can support in the business, rather than waiting to be told.

And, they want someone who can:

- ☑ **Setup, manage and strategically use a shopping cart system** to simplify and automate tasks.
- ☑ **Format and distribute broadcasts** such as, ezines, newsletters and announcements - and consider ways to measure their effectiveness via link tracking and open stats
- ☑ **Setup and completely automate online teleclass registrations** - from registration to post-class follow up.
- ☑ **Setup and maintain blog posts** for them, as part of their overall online strategy.
- ☑ **Assist with creating audio and written products** and setting them up to sell on a website.

- ☑ Support them with **attracting website traffic and list building activities.**
- ☑ Manage email based **customer service inquiries effectively.**

CHAPTER NINE

Continuing to Learn

$\mathcal{W}$hether you have a new business or a business filled with clients, you need to stay on top of the current trends and technology affecting your target market so you can continue sharpening your own VA skills.

According to the VANetworking.com Survey, about 20% of VAs indicated they had Online VA Training and a little more than 50% experienced on the job training. Visit http://www.vanetworking.com/survey/ for additional details.

There are hundreds of VA training programs available on the Internet and even in local community colleges today. Many of these programs focus on topics related to starting a Virtual Assistant business and include training in how to name a business, build a website, set up the office and basic administrative skills. However, all too often I have seen VAs graduate from their training feeling completely overwhelmed and frustrated with not being able to find and keep clients.

I have not found many programs that will fully equip a Virtual Assistant with the key skills needed to effectively build a business with great clients.

Why?

Because these programs are often general in nature. They provide VAs with general administrative skills that, in most cases, do not solve the specific challenges faced by potential clients.

Too often I have seen Virtual Assistants spend thousands of dollars on a VA program, only to be left with very little information on how to find and retain clients to build their business and generate revenue.

In fact, I've spoken with 'seasoned' Virtual Assistants who have said if they were to start again, they would invest in specific training related to determining their target market, identifying their challenges and learning the skills and technology required to offer a solution to these challenges.

In order to find and retain clients, you need to posses the skills that will provide a solution to their problem.

As a professional, this means you still must have the traditional 'business' pieces in place such as a professional website, business name, phone number, office equipment, software etc. However the skills required by your target market are what will build your business, get clients and generate revenue.

In previous chapters we spent time researching our target market and identifying their specific challenges. To determine what kind of training to invest in, consider if your skills meet and exceed what is required by your target market.

For example, in the coaching community many coaches want to create online products and have them available to sell on their website. They want website visitors to experience a professional, seamless and secure way to enter their credit card details and automatically receive the product they purchased, as well as additional details. In this case, they need a VA who is familiar with how to implement a shopping cart and autoresponder program. If you are unfamiliar with how to use a shopping cart program, investing in shopping cart training should be a consideration. By adding this skill to your repertoire, you will increase the interest of potential clients within your target market who need this support.

WHERE DO YOU FIND SKILL-BASED TRAINING?

Skill-based training can be hard to find.

Below are some suggestions to help you find training in specific areas:

1. Check out the "Hot Skills VA Training Program" My partner Tina and I offered this program annually and it is now also available as a self-study program. It includes various audio recordings, checklists and notes to support you in learning specific skills required by VAs who support coaches, trainers, consultants, speakers and authors. Check out **www.HotSkillsVATraining.com**

2. Reach out to your fellow VAs. Connect with your VA colleagues and others in your VA community and ask where they learned the skills you're interested in gaining. Perhaps they can refer you to a program or resource that offers what you're looking for.

3. Research online. There are various online websites that offer courses and workshops. They may not be VA specific programs, but may offer the training you're looking for.

4. Check out program tutorials, sign up for free trials and contact support with your questions. Take advantage of the resources offered by many programs available on the Internet. Sign up for a trial, experiment with the program, call support, check out the help files and investigate how you can make things work. In most cases, you can't do anything "wrong" in the trial that will create any kind of disaster so take advantage of trial and error learning.

5. Get a VA mentor. Is there a VA you admire or one that has the skills you're looking for? Perhaps they would be willing to mentor, coach or train you (or perhaps know someone who would).

By investing in yourself to learn the skills needed by your target market, you will:

- Feel more confident.
- Show your clients you have what they need.
- Offer an expertise that many other VAs may not offer.
- Specialize in a particular area (which may lead to increasing your rates).
- Limit the number of clients you work with.
- Build a more successful, and more satisfying business.
- Set yourself apart from other VAs.

My Story...

When I started my Virtual Assistant business in 2003, I looked into various VA programs available online. I didn't have a huge training budget available and I didn't feel these programs were right for me at the time. I decided I was going to get started on my business and then decide on what kind of training I wanted to invest in. At the time, my background included years of high-level administrative experience, but I knew nothing about online technology (I didn't even know what a shopping cart was!)

As I learned more about the challenges faced by my target market, I saw a pattern in the technology they needed support with. I was also fortunate to work with a client who trusted me to be 'let me loose' in her shopping cart account. She would let me know what she needed and I would log into the account and figure out how to get the task done.

I took advantage of everything I could – I called support, reviewed the tutorials, opened a trial account of my own and experimented on how to use as many of the features as I could.

I became very skilled at using the shopping cart, manipulating the features to do what I needed them to do. In the process of completely automating several tasks for my client I was also providing a great return on my client's investment of the program.

Within a short time, my profile as a 'shopping cart expert' grew and I attracted referrals and requests from new clients who needed help with setting up, customizing and utilizing features within the shopping cart.

I did the same with other programs that contributed to automating tasks within a business such as various broadcasting and autoresponder programs.

The "trial and error" type of training works well for me -- I learn best by experimenting and learning how the technology works. I do my best when I understand how to strategically apply the tool, rather than simply knowing where to point and click.

Decide what works best for you and invest in yourself. Nothing is more important than feeling confident and up-to-date on your skills. It may cost you money, but if you choose the right kind of training, you will reap the rewards from what you learned within the program.

YOU'RE DONE!

I hope you have enjoyed this book and I also hope you will feel inspired and empowered to implement even a handful of the strategies I've written about. I know that, if you do, it will make a big difference in the success of your business – it did in my business.

These steps are the exact ones that have led me to where I am today. In many cases, I was not aware of how my actions impacted my success and the success of my clients. Through thoughtful discussions with clients and colleagues, I was told about things I did that made a difference to my clients. However, it wasn't until the last three years that I could really define what those things were and how I did them.

I hope the tools, resources, strategies and tips I have outlined will prove to be the tools you need to help you also succeed. I firmly believe every Virtual Assistant can be successful. There is no better time to identify your target market, apply your skills, exercise your mindset, and build your client base. The business community awaits you.

Whatever the goals you want to achieve with owning and operating your VA business, know that it is possible. The opportunities far exceed the number of Virtual Assistants. The profession and clients await you.

Starting my VA business in 2003 was one of the best decisions I have made. Even though I have endured various challenges, sleepless nights, stress and frustration I wouldn't change my experiences for anything. My business has allowed me (with the support of my family) to enjoy flexible time with my children while continuing my career and contributing financially to my family. I feel blessed to be with my children, participating with them and enjoying them each day while earning a living doing what I love to do.

Thank you for reading My Story. I hope it may contribute, even if only in a small way, to your own success story.

APPENDIX

VA / Women Entrepreneur Organizations Online

Alliance for Virtual Businesses	www.allianceforvirtualbiz.com
Association of Administrative Assistants of Canada	www.aaa.ca
Canadian Entrepreneurial Women	www.womennet.ca
Canadian Virtual Assistant Connection	www.cvac.ca
CVAN (Canadian Virtual Assistants Network)	www.canadianva.net
The Canadian Virtual Assistant	www.canadianvirtualassistant.com
Canadian Women's Business Network	www.cdnbizwomen.com
Digital Women	www.digital-women.com
Digital Eve	www.digitaleve.org
Global Association of Virtual Assistants (GAVA)	www.gava.org
International Association of Virtual Office Assistants (IAVOA)	www.iavoa.com
International Virtual Assistants Association (IVAA)	www.ivaa.org

National Virtual Assistants Society	www.nvas.org
International Association of Administrative Professionals	www.iaap-hq.org
International Real Estate Assistant Association	www.ireaa.ca
National Association of Women Business Owners	www.nawbo.org
Online International Virtual Assistants Convention	www.oivac.com
VANetworking	www.VANetworking.com
Virtual Assistant Certification	www.vacertification.com
Virtual Assistance U	www.virtualassistanceu.com
Virtual Assistant Chamber of Commerce	www.virtualassistantnetworking.com

Sample Client Agreement

DATE

CLIENT SERVICES AGREEMENT

between

VA COMPANY NAME

and

CLIENT NAME (the "Client")

The following constitutes a binding letter of agreement between VA COMPANY NAME, a LOCATION company, and CLIENT NAME (the "Client"), for good and valuable consideration the sufficiency of which is hereby acknowledged:

TASKS/DUTIES

As initially discussed via telephone, VA COMPANY NAME or its designee agrees to perform on behalf of the Client the following tasks:

- TASKS OUTLINED

PRICE FOR SERVICES:
Packages discussed:

-

COMMUNICATION:
The Client agrees to (i) provide clear and specific direction regarding tasks that VA COMPANY NAME shall perform, along with pertinent deadline and other information, (ii) provide prompt additional information to VA COMPANY NAME, if requested, in order to speed the completion of any task and (iii) provide adequate supervision of any task to be performed to such an extent so that such task could be repeated with little or no supervision. Each of VA COMPANY NAME and the Client agree that honest and forthright communication will be maintained with each other AT ALL TIMES.

PROVISION OF WORK:
VA COMPANY NAME is committed to learning and growing with your business and providing you with the best possible service. We strive to always give our honest, best efforts.

CONFIDENTIALITY:
Each of VA COMPANY NAME and the Client agree to never disclose, directly or indirectly, unless required by law, any information concerning each other's business or projects, _provided_ that VA COMPANY NAME may make any disclosure that is part of any marketing or publicity efforts implemented on behalf of, and expressly approved by, the Client.

FEES/REMUNERATION:

All remuneration with respect to this agreement will take place in United States dollars. Please initial the package that you would like to start with:

DETAILS ABOUT FEES

EXPENSES:

Unless otherwise agreed, all reasonable expenses documented and incurred in the provision of certain services will be charged to the Client, such as, office supplies, postage and long distance calls with the Client's consent.

VA COMPANY NAME is an independent contractor and is solely responsible for payment of any income or other taxes on the amounts received from the Client.

RE-EVALUATION OF FEES/SERVICES:

The Client and VA COMPANY NAME agree to re-visit and discuss (i) the fees associated with increased requests for service and for associated expenses and (ii) the terms of this agreement to insure such terms accurately reflect the understanding between the parties on at least a semi-annual basis.

DISSOLUTION OF AGREEMENT:

Either party may terminate this agreement upon 30 calendar days written notice to the other. All monies owed to VA COMPANY NAME in respect of tasks in process at the time the termination notice is delivered shall be paid by the end of the 30 day period. Once such final payment is made, any and all files/records belonging to the

Client shall be returned and all electronic information pertaining to the Client shall be deleted from VA COMPANY NAME data files.

NON-DISPARAGEMENT:

The parties and any of their affiliates, officers or directors agree that they shall not make any false, defamatory or disparaging statements about the other party or any of its affiliates, officers or directors.

ENTIRE AGREEMENT/MODIFICATION:

This Agreement embodies the entire agreement and understanding of the parties in respect of the subject matter of this Agreement, and supersedes and replaces in its entirety all prior agreements, understandings and commitments with respect to such subject matter. This Agreement may not be changed orally but only by an agreement in writing agreed to by the parties.

BEST EFFORTS:

The parties hereto shall use their best efforts to promptly take, or cause to be taken, all actions necessary or advisable to carry out the purposes of this Agreement, including, without limitation, the execution of additional instruments by their directors or officers, as well as any other reasonable action requested by the other party.

LIMITATION OF LIABILITY/EXCLUSIVE REMEDY:

VA COMPANY NAME entire liability for any damages which may arise hereunder, for any cause whatsoever, and regardless of the form of action, whether in contract or in tort, including its negligence, or otherwise, shall be limited to money damages in an amount equal to the lesser of (a) actual direct damages or (b) the total price actually paid by the Client to VA COMPANY NAME for the tasks set forth herein.

IN NO EVENT WILL VA COMPANY NAME BE LIABLE FOR ANY SPECIAL, INDIRECT, INCIDENTAL, OR CONSEQUENTIAL DAMAGES, INCLUDING BUT NOT LIMITED TO, FOR ANY LOSS OF BUSINESS OR PROSPECTIVE BUSINESS OPPORTUNITIES, PROFITS, SAVINGS, INFORMATION, USE OR OTHER COMMERCIAL OR ECONOMIC LOSS, EVEN IF VA COMPANY NAME HAS BEEN ADVISED OF THE POSSIBILITY OF SUCH DAMAGES.

NO SET-OFF:

Any payments paid by the Client under this Agreement shall not be subject to set-off and shall be increased by the amount, if any, of any taxes (other than income taxes) or other governmental charges levied in respect of such payments, so that VA COMPANY NAME is made whole for such taxes or charges.

IN WITNESS WHEREOF, the parties hereto have caused this Agreement to be executed by their respective duly authorized representatives as of the date set forth above.

VA COMPANY NAME

_____

VA COMPANY OWNER NAME   Date

_____

CLIENT NAME   Date

_____

The Communication Plan

The Communication Plan

Communication is a vital component to any relationship. Without good communication, a relationship is bound to lack success. I can't stress enough how important it is to have a good communication plan in place with your client. This doesn't need to be a formal document. It's meant to be a discussion, so both parties are aware of how the relationship will move forward.

Everyone has different work styles and levels of flexibility in their business. By discussing how you will each communicate with each other, you will avoid potentially frustrating situations and have a more productive relationship.

When discussing a communication plan with your client, consider the following:

- **Working hours**
  - Standard hours of operation
  - Best time to reach each other
- **Preferred methods of communication**
  - Will you communicate mostly through email or by phone? (I recommend talking live at least once a month and managing communication around projects/tasks via email. Some people prefer to have a weekly call as

well).

- **Establishing monthly goals**
  - What are the top 3 projects of the month? Top priorities? Upcoming deadlines?
- **Touch Base Weekly**
  - Touching base on the status of projects for the month keeps everyone on the same page. Even if there has been no work on a project that week, I often just touch base to say, "on hold" or whatever it happens to be.
- **Keep each email to one topic only**
  - By keeping each email to one topic only, it allows for easier response and sorting of the tasks/projects in your inbox.
- **Clarity on requests & deadlines**
  - Share as much as possible and be clear about expectations: when you need it/deadlines; budget; when to consult or advise of status, etc. It's better to over communicate, especially in the early stages of working together.
- **Keep a "master project" list**
  - It's helpful to have a list that identifies the tasks related to a large project and who is responsible for what. Also include deadlines and commitments.
- **Be realistic about time expectations**
  - Talk about turnaround time for projects, emails, articles, etc. Consider planning ahead rather than working on continuously rushed projects

By discussing these topics with your client, you are much more likely to have a successful, long-term relationship with your client. It also shows your client that you are serious about working with them and want to have a positive impact on their business.

Sample Press Release

Virtual Assistants Learn the "Hot" Skills Business Owners Want

The Virtual Assistant profession is growing annually. VA's across the globe are spending thousands of dollars on training, yet online-based business owners claim there is a shortage of VA's with the right skills.

> *"There is a mismatch between available Virtual Assistants and the business owners who want to hire them. There are many capable and eager Virtual Assistants who are struggling to find (and keep) new clients yet there are online-based business owners who are struggling to find Virtual Assistants with the right skills to support their business needs. The result is an unwin-unwin situation."*
> ~ Tina Forsyth, Partner of the Multiple Streams Team, a leader in matching business owners with qualified Virtual Assistant support.

Over the last 24 months, I have spoken with almost 400 business owners who indicated to me what they desperately want from their VAs and what they are willing to pay for.

To respond to this need my partner, Tina Forsyth, and I are launching a "Hot Virtual Skills Training Program" for Virtual Assistants who want to expand their skill set and never go without clients again. This has been created specifically for the VA who is interested in working with coaches, consultants, authors, speakers, online-based business and who has a technical knack for, and enjoyment of, working online.

The program consists of 12 sessions over 6 weeks and has been priced affordably. Items covered range from technical online skills shopping cart administration, to setting up products/programs for sale to developing a marketing mindset – taking initiative with current clients and using it to attract and retain high-level clients.

For VA's needing help in getting their business started – this program is not for you. This is strictly a skills building course that will provide the essential skills and mindset business owners are looking for.

For more information about the upcoming Hot Virtual Skills Training program visit: **www.HotSkillsVATraining.com**

About the Hot Virtual Skills Training

This program is led by Cindy Greenway and Tina Forsyth of
www.GrowYourVABiz.com and the Multiple Streams Team,
a leader in matching business owners with qualified Virtual
Assistant support.

Contact Information:
Cindy Greenway / Tina Forsyth
http://www.MultipleStreamsTeam.com
http://www.GrowYourVABiz.com
team@growyourvabiz.com

Sample Client Application Form

(Business owners complete this form when applying for help with the Multiple Streams Team:
www.MultipleStreamsTeam.com/clientapplication.html)

Need a Great Virtual Assistant?

If you're looking for help with your business, then you've come to the right place.

The Multiple Streams Team, led by "yours truly" Cindy Greenway, specializes in providing support to coaches, consultants and other professionals. Let us find the person that can best assist you.

The first step is to let us know what you would like help with. To assist us in determining your needs, please complete the form below.

Email Address:

Name:

Phone:

Website:

Time Zone:

Please check everything that you need assistance with. This

will help us to identify the Virtual Assistant(s) that offers expertise in this area.

- [ ] Shopping Cart Administration
- [ ] Website Design
- [ ] Website Maintenance/Editing
- [ ] Ezine Broadcasting/Autoresponders
- [ ] Customer Service
- [ ] Graphic Design
- [ ] Writing/Editing
- [ ] Audio/Video Editing
- [ ] Blog Setup/Customization
- [ ] Transcription
- [ ] Bookkeeping
- [ ] Online Research
- [ ] Word Processing
- [ ] Powerpoint Presentations
- [ ] Event Management
- [ ] Project Management
- [ ] Database Management
- [ ] Article Submission
- [ ] Search Engine Marketing
- [ ] Anything Else? List Below:

Tell us a bit about your business. What do you offer? Who is your market?

Do you have any specific projects/tasks that you would like to complete with the assistance of a Virtual Assistant? i.e. Creating a website or writing an ebook.

Who do you currently have on staff or contract? And what do they do for you? i.e. Web Designers, other VAs, etc.

How many hours help do you anticipate needing each month from a VA? (Note: based on high demand for our services, clients, with a minimum need of 10 hours a month with be prioritized.)

Rates vary depending on the tasks. What is your monthly budget for VA help? (in USD)

Feel free to share anything else that you would like us to know about you and your business.

How did you hear about the Multiple Streams Team? Who referred you?

101 Ways to Boost Business with a Virtual Assistant

PINK SPOON DEVELOPMENT & IMPLEMENTATION
- Proofread your Pink Spoon
- Format your Pink Spoon
- Set up the delivery of your Pink Spoon (in your shopping cart or autoresponder program)
- Post the Pink Spoon sign up form on your website
- Assist in drafting text and designing thank you webpage where people will be directed to once they sign up for your Pink Spoon
- Connect with previous customers/clients etc. to request testimonials
- Create a simple Pink Spoon webpage (or work in collaboration with web designer)
- Arrange hosting of your Pink Spoon webpage

WEBSITE MAINTENANCE
- Make simple updates to your website (or work in collaboration with web designer)
- Monitor website traffic and conversion
- Review website on a monthly basis to check for broken links, old data
- Create and add opt-in forms for Pink Spoon sign up, teleclass registration etc.

BLOG PROMOTION & MAINTENANCE

- Set up blog (free blog with minimal customization) or communicating with blog designer
- Post content to your blog
- Research places to submit your blog to
- Research other blogs to post and link to
- Submit postings to other blogs (previous communication/approval required)

SHOPPING CART MAINTENANCE

- Set up your shopping cart system
- Link you merchant account to your shopping cart
- Customize your shopping cart to include your logo, contact details, address etc.

PRODUCT DEVELOPMENT & DELIVERY

- Help in the development of your written and audio products
- Research copywriters, book editors, book publishers, graphic designers
- Set up new products in your shopping cart and link them appropriately to your website
- Set up electronic products to be delivered electronically once paid for by the customer
- Assist in drafting text for thank you webpage where people will be directed to once they purchase a product
- Draft and implement autoresponder(s) for each product available for sale
- Transcription of audio products to create written product
- Connect with graphic designer to create appropriate image for product (ebook cover etc.)
- Research and set up fulfillment house for shipping of products
- Submit product orders for fulfillment

AUTORESPONDER DEVELOPMENT & DELIVERY

- Draft and create autoresponders in your shopping cart for all products, teleclass signups etc.
- Create sign up forms to place on your website

TELECLASS MAINTENANCE & SUPPORT

- Schedule/reserve teleclass bridge line
- Draft teleclass announcement, reminders, follow up emails related to teleclass and include important information such as bridge line, date/time, time zones, teleclass topic, teleclass protocol,
- Answer any inquiries as to time zone, will call be recorded, will recording be available etc.
- Provide you with a summary prior to the teleclass with important details - teleclass date/time, topic, summary, how many registered, audio recording details
- Post audio recordings to website
- Follow up with registrants with audio recording information and other follow up details

EZINE/NEWSLETTER DEVELOPMENT & DELIVERY

- Proofread your ezine, provide suggestions and ensure important information is included
- Draft up simple parts of your ezine for your review
- Format your ezine broadcast using ezine delivery program (Constant Contact, aWeber etc.)
- Send your ezine broadcast - ensuring links, images and other items are done correctly
- Use tracking links within the ezine copy to track click throughs and conversion of sales versus click throughs etc.

LIST BUILDING

- Create an email signature file that includes link to website and Pink Spoon
- Attend network events with you or on your behalf (local VAs)
- Develop a broadcast schedule - include blog postings, ezine, reminder notices etc. and remind you of "due dates"
- Set up a tell a friend account
- Implement the tell a friend option on your website

ARTICLES

- Proofread your articles
- Distribute your articles online
- Track where articles are successfully posted to online

JOINT VENTURES

- Research joint venture partners
- Research where your niche market "hangs out" on the Internet
- Assisting in tracking joint venture activity
- Communicate with joint venture partners regularly (once relationship established)

PRESS RELEASES

- Assist in drafting and proofreading press releases
- Submit your press releases online
- Contact television, radio, newspapers, magazines to submit press release/information of interest
- Sign up to receive Google Alerts and monitor specific keywords/competitors

SPEAKING (SEE ALSO EVENT MANAGEMENT)

- Research organizations within your niche market that you would like to speak to
- Create a master list of places that you can speak to and how to submit your speaker package
- Create a speaker package with the appropriate information (bio, picture, topics etc.)
- Submit a speaker package on your behalf to organizations and follow up with appropriate people
- Assist with creating any presentation materials for your speaking engagements
- Help brainstorm how to make the most of the speaking engagement - how to collect names/contact information
- Assist with live presentation recording details (videographer etc.)
- Create a feedback form to use at the presentation
- Follow up with presentation attendees after event
- Enter new leads into the main database
- Follow up with presentation attendees by phone to tell them about the products/services they expressed interest in

TARGET MARKET RESEARCH

- Research online groups for your target market
- Sign up, receive, review and response (where appropriate) to online group messages with specific content
- Research other places where your target market "hangs out" - both online and offline

EVENT MANAGEMENT (SEE ALSO SPEAKING)
- Researching locations to hold a live event
- Organize travel, hotel, transportation arrangements
- Venue arrangements - seating arrangements, beverages, audio/ visual equipment
- Research caterers, florists etc.
- Make appropriate arrangements for copying of presentation material, shipping of product
- Assist in the marketing of the event
- Provide location directions to registrants
- Research local media outlets in event location - radio, television, newspaper - collecting appropriate names, contact information, preferred method of how to receive press release
- Draft press release to submit to media outlets
- Follow up with media outlets to get more attention for the event
- Connect with joint venture partners to assist in the promotion of the event
- Connect with affiliate partners to assist in the promotion of the event
- ...See speaking items above also

AFFILIATE PROGRAM MAINTENANCE
- Set up an affiliate program
- Connect with graphic designers to create promotional material (banners etc.) for affiliates
- Develop copy that affiliates can use to promote product
- Manage affiliate program - connect with affiliates, answer questions/provide support
- Keep in touch with affiliates - tips on ways to promote product etc.

CUSTOMER SUPPORT / ADMINISTRATIVE

- Check your voicemail messages and respond to standard inquiries or providing you with details where appropriate
- Provide customer support, billing support and trouble shooting to customers, clients etc.
- Set up recurring billing for clients
- Schedule your client appointments
- Set up an online calendar so people can schedule appointments with you
- Send out birthday cards or other appreciation cards on your behalf
- Reporting of monthly sales, revenues, expenses
- Implementation of online systems (online calendar, membership software, shopping cart etc.)
- Provide support on how to organize email inbox, document folders etc.
- Manage customer support for your membership group
- Screen emails - sending you only what you need to see
- Pay your bills online or set up recurring payments
- Manage projects/tasks/priorities
- Remind you of important dates/deadlines
- Take notes during calls to capture important information